Art In Time

Cole Swensen   Art In Time

Nightboat Books New York

ISBN: 978-1-64362-037-4

Design and typesetting by Rissa Hochberger
Text set in Folio

Cover Art: Cécile Beau, *Suma*, wood, varied vegetation, digital recording, 2010.
Courtesy of the artist.

Cataloging-in-publication data is available from
the Library of Congress

Nightboat Books
New York
www.nightboat.org

Contents

"The aim of this book is to change *landscape* from a noun to a verb."

WJT Mitchell, from *Landscape and Power*

" … to recapture the structure of the landscape as an emerging organism."

Merleau-Ponty, from "Cezanne's Doubt"

Introduction
An Argument Against Timeless Art

I recently stayed at a place on the edge of a valley with an exceptionally stunning view—which made me question what I meant by a *view* and what might make one stunning or not—and what either might have to do with landscape and the way that that concept is deployed in the western world.

It struck me that what made it stunning was something about its vastness, which made me ask what vastness is—perhaps some kind of sensible evidence of, and thus recognition of, the endlessness of the world. And that vastness seemed to act as a catalyst. Because of it, every time I walked out into the view, I, for a split-second, participated that endlessness, was aware of myself as an integral part of it. Suddenly, albeit only very briefly, I wasn't looking at it; I *was* it.

An instant later, I returned to the common human sensation of being a body looking out on a scene that I then walked into, but though I was now physically entering the view, I felt that I was, ironically, less a part of it.

I think that split-second sensation of fusion with the world occurs to many people, perhaps even to most, but so quickly that we're usually not aware of it, and yet a vestige of that fusion, that complete participation, remains, and it alters one's relationship to the world. That fusion of seer and seen/scene is, I believe, what the landscape artists discussed in the following pieces are trying—consciously or not—to capture.

These artists—again, intentionally or not—have engaged the landscape genre in a fluid way, a way that puts the landscape back into motion, and in doing so, they have found alternatives to some of the presumptions and practices of landscape art common to Euro-centric contexts, such as the use of linear perspective, in which the proper viewing position can only be occupied by one person at a time, thus implicitly supporting hierarchical social and political systems and the regimes of appropriation, colonization, and exclusion that go with them.

A substantial body of western landscape theory written over the past thirty+ years has critiqued the genre's reinforcement of binaries such as inside/outside, subject/object, and culture/nature. Such binaries are part of the ideological approach through which landscape art can reduce a complex network of animal, vegetal, and mineral interactions to a static ornament, reinforcing a sense of human power over "nature," imposing specific cultural values, and/or claiming or exercising control. Such a stance projects human interests and desires so thoroughly that they effectively anthropomorphize the world, subjugating its non-human elements to humans' will to turn the world to our uses and/or reflect our domination of (and imagined separation from) the "natural" world.

And yet, throughout the centuries, various artists have taken quite different approaches, implicitly or explicitly advocating relationships with the earth based on collaboration rather than domination, conversation rather than control. Achieved through variations on conventional depictions of the world around them, such works, rather than standing back and looking at that world, instead participate in it, thus keeping something of the vital motion of the moment intact.

That motion is not only spatial, but also temporal. In the process of presenting space in dynamic flow, these works also acknowledge the fluidity of time. They are not interested in being "timeless," an epithet often applied to works marked by a distilled quality that they've only achieved at the expense of remaining disengaged from their own moment; instead, these works insist on specificity, on particularity; in short, they advocate an art *in time*, in all the possible meanings of that term—an art conjugated into the present, and in time to do something about that present. If art is the verb in the grammar of culture, it's those works of art in the active tenses that have the most potential to play a role in keeping that culture responsive to its immediate demands and needs.

As the terms *inherently* and *implicitly* suggest, none of these artists has, to my knowledge, ever suggested that they see their works along these lines. These are qualities and values that I find in them, and yet I think that what I'm proposing in each case is neither inaccurate nor misleading. These artists have all found ways through landscape to become an active element in the view and its viewing, with viewer and view mutually constructing each other, thus encouraging an increased recognition of our

3

belonging to, participating in, and thus being responsible to and for the earth.

All the works referenced can easily be found on the Internet.

4

Willem de Kooning
Composed Windows

Field: if there's a woman in a garden, there's a field in shredded
color or a woman in an arc of garden peeling backward. If there's
a field, it's only color outward, if the body of the garden were ever
hurled open, its howl of color tearing the horizon into hundreds
of days
each day
Willem de Kooning
stowed away
on a British freighter heading for Argentina
(hiding in the engine room for the twelve days it took to cross the
Atlantic) and disembarked at Newport News in 1926, his mother
having once again violently assaulted him, and it was, he decided,
time to become bohemian.

Field: a flag of erasure, one life becomes another, apparently
greener. Apparently putting the field directly in the center, de
Kooning wandered the upward farther, working as a house painter
and a bit for the WPA.

It was summer: *Pink Landscape* 1938: it was morning and it was going to stay that way.

In a re-examination of the nature of territory, de Kooning came to see a different way of reading contour—the possibility of a "landscape of the body." In the summer of 1948, he was invited to teach at Black Mountain as a last-minute replacement for a painter who had cancelled due to illness.

And a good thing it was, said Elaine; they were totally broke with nothing looking hopeful. A photo shows Willem slightly fragile and fierce against a background that would be vividly green if it weren't in black & white against all of rolling North Carolina.

Asheville, 1948, great height as the field backs up, great in its white and climbs   so inhabited   from the inside, a body exudes its own landscape. De Kooning no longer worried about the source of the curve, the flight of the line. If there's a line that flies and the following eye, if the eye should follow a line of hills until a figure turns around and is caught as the background—such enormous distance inflicted—ignites the sky.

Bolton Landing, 1957, the lake stretching impossibly into sight, standing on the shore with David Smith, the light coming back to strike the side of a boathouse or pier behind them throwing the whole into relief against the brilliant water creating its own sun crossing in its pattern.

By the late 50s he was getting increasingly abstract, creating landscapes he referred to as pastoral and parkway. *Artists have no pasts*, he said, and *Bless your heart* when he meant goodbye.

At times de Kooning kept his paintings from drying too quickly by covering them with newspapers at times leaving a ghost trace of the news sifting across the surface of the picture.

At times de Kooning would paint all day and then scrape the whole thing down at the end and in the morning begin again with the remains, a new ghost as a floating difference that will surface later in the eye of the viewer, which is also always historically layered.

Returning to Europe for several months in black and white, 1959 to 1960: *Villa Borghese*. He walked on his hands all across Rome, his hands held on.

Also in 1960, he painted *Door to the River*, this time on his way to and from East Hampton with house-painters' brushes, painting the door open.

In 1961, he began work on a new studio in Springs, Long Island. A 1962 photo by Hans Namuth shows him standing in an enormous excavated space with a line of trees behind. There are tracks from heavy machinery at his feet, and most of the trees are bare.

In just a few weeks, leaves will create a wall of green extending beyond the photo's frame farther than the eye can see. A few years later, he executed a series of paintings on actual doors purchased for the purpose, which made the works necessarily tall and narrow, the opposite of a landscape's proportions, and though they were, in fact, compositions based on women, we sense in them a landscape deepened by the constraint of the format, which in turn awakens, in the center of each work, a source of sky.

He is said to have kept an "unnaturally" neat studio composed largely of windows, including a skylight 40 feet wide, a roof of sheer sight.

And though he couldn't see the sea, it wasn't far away—*The North Atlantic Light*, 1977 with a child's sailboat at the center of a blue that stutters through a rehearsal of convergent color, making echolocation a medium of figuration, and so, on can go the boat into its storm.

8

Rosa Bonheur
Animals with Landscape

Ruskin compared her to a zookeeper.

All her life, she lived with the animals she painted—
hares   horses   huge bulls   the sun filtering through leaves   the gold falling on all sides washing over the face, the gold on the hooves   and the hooves on the *pristine paths of snow*   through Fontainebleau marked also by the passage of deer Looking out from there, the eye drawing back the leaves, the eye drawing bare trees.

On the one hand, Rosa Bonheur literally animated her landscapes with the animals that she loved, while on the other, the larger, she often masked it; the big, shaggy bodies of two rams, for instance, covering at least three-quarters of the canvas, rendering invisible the river in the distance, and the distance along with it.

Or a line of oxen blocking out the world, and so becoming the world, telling Ruskin that she didn't *want* to paint every hair of the hide, *even a photograph wouldn't do that*. Every hair of her gazelle, of her mouflon, of her chamois, of her yak. Her wild boar, squirrel, and eagle—and all were usually plural. Her cats.

She strove to capture their expressions so precisely because she believed that the gaze gives away the soul. And that they gave theirs freely—the ferrets, lizards, foxes, and parrots, and sometimes a person or two—usually Nathalie.

Rosa Bonheur lived her entire adult life with her oldest friend, Nathalie Micus, also a painter, and Micus' mother, Henriette, both of them as determined as Bonheur to *"relever la femme."* Bonheur had the gift of being close, and to almost everything at once. Though her favorites were the sheep—up to 50 at a time.

Sheep Shearers: pencil, undated, measured; it's a series of studies, so the men are scattered, unrelated across the paper, and affectionate; they hold the animals gently, and in one, the sheep raises her head, looking up at the man with a question in mind. *We may not always understand them, but they always understand us.* Though oddly enough, she also hunted.

The next piece in the catalogue offers a striking contrast to the drawing's meticulous care. *Landscape with Animals*, oil on panel, also undated and entirely devoid of detail; she is, at this point, just blocking out the shapes and juxtaposing the fields of color, ready at any moment to shift a vaguely sheep-shaped patch of white or what might become a shepherd in response to the demands of rhythm.

Back to the souls of animals: she disagreed entirely with Descartes and his view of animals as pure machines, noting instead the metempsychosis at the moment of death, the sound of a letter slipping out of its envelope or slipping back in.

And if the land in its shapes, too has a soul, and is also always plural, and always moving off beyond itself, or running, if a river runs across it in its forces—and what happens to a landscape when an animal enters? Creating a sudden gesture of color and heat. Becoming the gesture, the answer to space. Space in the shape of a stag, a swan, a lamb, a crow, and perfectly exactly filled out to its edges with the larger presence of breath.

And the world beyond simply melts, becomes a field of fusing greens, a sweeping brush of tree into meadow, hedgerow, and grove—a wash of the thriving; things so entirely living need no form. And nothing can be more alive than green, not a thing, but another force, like gravity or electromagnetism; she let it loose and unleashed a streak that wanders, winding around the animals, holding them in.

The term *peinture animalière* was invented by Théophile Gautier in 1855, effectively inaugurating a genre spliced between portrait and landscape. Though usually in a landscape format, it's the living being or beings that dominate, thus it counters the concept of landscape, but also that of portraiture, as it focuses on the entire body, as if an animal's every inch held the capacity for the kind of expressivity that in the human is restricted to the face.

Such works are also sometimes referred to as *paysages animés*, animated landscapes, landscape as living being, as itself animal—implying that it breathes, seethes, is composed of systems, circulatory, nervous, etc., with senses.

Ploughing in the Nivernais, 1849, her first government commission, one year after the February Revolution, with its consequent shift in social attention, is a scene possibly suggested by the opening of George Sand's 1846 novel *The Devil's Pool*, focusing, muscular, on the eye; the second ox from the right inclines his head toward the painter, where you and I are now standing. The eye is alive, not just with the life of the animal but with a life of its own—in that eye we are present and are the present time

and indignant and much more engaged than the men, who are slightly misshapen and lacking detail—their eyes, for instance, can't really be seen in the shadow of a hat or at the back of the line or not seeing a thing.

Even earlier: *Two Rabbits*, 1840, with exceptionally long and shapely ears, the one on the left sniffing a carrot as though suspecting a trap. A parsnip lounges off to the side. This is one of two paintings that her father urged her to send to the 1841 salon; it was her first attempt, and both were accepted.

Though not widely remembered today, Rosa Bonheur was arguably the most celebrated artist of her time, rowing around the Lake of the Carp at Fontainebleau with the Empress Eugènie, Eugènie herself at the oars . . . receiving honors from countries all over Europe and beyond, though the one of which she was the most proud was the *Légion d'honneur*, which the Empress presented to her in person in 1865. She was the first female artist ever to receive it.

She lived an independent life, insisted on it, never married, wore trousers—which required the permission of the police at the time—and traveled widely, bringing a wealth of images back from her trips:

Morning fog and up through fog, the way things come up through fog, somehow seeming closer as they grow yet more faint. They retain the ghostly—you can see the ghost inside them, a morning in Scotland, several cows, but because of the fog, they can't settle into a finite number. Became *Morning in the Highlands*, 1857.

And another, a lake across which the cattle swam on their way to the annual market at Falkirk, some of them, almost drowning, held above the water's surface by their horns by men rowing alongside them in boats. Became *The Boat*, 1856.

And later, on the same trip, another lake singing in the dark, across a lake around a lake, the way the dark makes the walk, and farther on, we hear (Nathalie writing to her mother) *It was the only time I ever heard her sing.*

1850: in the Pyrenees, admiring the *grandiose savagery* of the mountains from the back of a horse that she and Nathalie shared in order to cut the cost. *You have no idea how hard it was not to bring back a sheep and a goat.* On a later trip, 1853, they did bring back an otter, who often snuck into the house and joined Henriette in bed.

Bonheur's whole family were artists: her father, a devoted Saint-Simonian, who abandoned his family for the cause, leaving Rosa with the firm conviction that a woman should never let herself become dependent on a man, and all her siblings—two brothers, a sister, and a half-brother—they were all painters except for one, who was a sculptor, and four of her seven nieces and nephews. They often painted or sculpted each other, often in the studio, often in the act of creating an animal.

In 1860, she bought the Chateau de By near Fontainebleau with its own forest, the light barely making its way through the overlapping layers of overlapping leaves. Studies of trees and of the structure of light, the tiny grains that dust over all things and the fragile sound as they settle on stone.

14

Rosa Bonheur: pink happiness; the joy of the flower, calling her stag Jacques, her lioness Fatma, her boar Kiki, and so on. Bonheur's animals are never metaphoric, never symbolic, always simply distinct individuals with proper names.

The power of that particularity dominates her work, for instance, the horses in *The Horse Fair*, 1853, with their coiled musculature that practically cracks the canvas, the violence inherent, could be considered a displacement of her own rebellious spirit, except for the individual expression in each horse's face, which instead suggests acute observation and a grasp of the irreducible actuality of each.

And there's a connection between her interest in "raising up the state of women" and her recognition of the souls and individualities of animals, as, of course, in 19th century France, both animals and women were entirely at the mercy of men. Often loved, yes, often deeply valued, but with a love and appreciation that could be revoked at any time and that did not suffer the need to be requited.

Which may also be related to her increasing drift beyond the domestic—animals largely separate from the human sphere. *Herd of Deer in a Forest*, 1898, the year before she died, each one looking in a slightly different direction, and, as in *Ploughing in the Nivernaise* from so many years earlier, one looks directly at her, seeming not to mind her presence.

After the Franco-Prussian war, it was lions (she had five in all, though not all at once), which amounted to a complex confluence of the domestic and the wild; thoroughly the latter, hers had all been transformed into the former. And mostly they didn't live very long, but they lived peacefully, affectionately, padding softly around the house and grounds, terrifying the guests.

Agnès Varda
Here There & Then Now

Landscape of rain
                    raining down a street.
                              People move more slowly in the rain
because suddenly they're anonymous
                                        which gives them more time.

I am in time. I'm old. I've been crossing time for years—

                    Landscape of later:
Rain raining down the house
                              reappearing on the windows of a train—
umbrellas and small sails—
                    the theater of the sea.

Varda said that her favorite landscape was the sea, having grown
up partly in Sète, on the southern coast of France where her first
film, *La Pointe Courte*, considered by many to be the beginning
of French New Wave cinema, takes place against a background
salted brittle

                    the splinter
                                      of air that crackles between them
out there
                    the boats
                                      just a liquid line of lighted windows,
a candle bright upon a table.

Landscape with island out window
                              with a window as large as the house
and its shadow.

18   Landscape of sand dunes
                              the sun cut into seagulls.
Landscape in the shape of a breeze.
                              Breeze in the shape of its trees.

She'd originally planned a career as a museum curator but got
intrigued with photography when taking a night class. Though
soon found, she said, too much silence in photos and not enough
time. Film as light in flight in time. She'd only seen a handful of
films in her life when she made her first one, which she says she
made by hand.

Landscape through which runs a river
                              both sides lined with trees
slightly therefore flowing green,
                              the bells strung between
follow in slight distance
                              etched onto the panes of an *orangerie*.

Landscape of evening
                    shadowing a park

Landscape of ventriloquist in nearby pavilion,
                              the land itself a voice
and the voice repeating:
                    My treasure
was a cedar. Landscape
                    of heart in water
of white shirts in a stream

of silence coming through a white sheet thrown over a chair—

Landscape of a sheet of sun made of bees.

Her first show was in 1954—her photographs mounted on shutters
and ladders in the courtyard of her new home in the rue Daguerre.
She later bought a hardware store in the same street to use as
her editing studio from which she sold her films on DVDs through
the window.

Landscape abandoned in a garden—
                    empty shoes
two grey and
                    two green. Fake wings. In the shadow
of a distant season
                    in which green reigns.

Landscape of distance
                    drawn on linen.

Landscape drawn out past the horizon.

Varda was born in 1928 in Belgium to a Greek father and a mother from all mothers who glean, who, like all films, are a matter of the past and a kite held aloft.

Les Glaneurs et la Glaneuse is, for many, particularly central to her œuvre—which is fitting, as all film is a gleaning—it gets only left-over light, that not absorbed by things, which makes us aware that the same principle determines all that we are and are not able to see.

Varda often focused on people often unheard—vagabonds, gleaners, cleaners, shopkeepers, villagers, with landscape framing, even enabling, character—Her late film *Visages, Villages* with the face of the French countryside moving smoothly behind, the one thing that binds all these otherwise disparate places and faces—

a landscape that opens
                          just like the faces
of the children going pale in the pouring light
                          of ripe wheat
blanchisserie of all is summer
                          in their glances
looking back in defiance
                          at the camera
so perhaps there really is
                          a heart in each small box
all so strikingly alike

                          the face fading back

and the heart now reduced to a sound
                                        keeping time.

Landscape with street on which wind—
                                        in which women lean in—
Landscape of a line of lights
                        down a street in a storm.

Landscape of a woman
                        holding up a lamp.
Landscape of a woman
                        succumbing to light.

Of a woman with weather streaked in stone.

Landscape of a woman
                        on a balcony hanging out a sheet.

A woman walks up the quai with a basket of laundry on her head.

Another woman resting
                        against the blade of her scythe.

Varda was also, all her life, an outspoken activist for women's
rights—and others'—her 1968 film on the Black Panthers—

Landscape as history
                        as a trajectory perpendicular to memory
Landscape of history
                        as a long row of rooms

with all their windows aligned
                passing their faces behind
their hands
       at the edge of the drapes.

Landscape as seeing
             the hand as a landscape
held up to the sunlight
          showing through.

Landscape of a hand
            reaching out
to take a box of matches
       off a shelf
that sees itself strike a match
          to light a candle at noon.

Candle that sees
         because a flame is a living thing.
Landscape as all
        that is living in the eye in range.
Landscape as living
       in the range of an eye.

The past doesn't mean
       so much to me because it's always here.

Scene of silence
       filling first the screen.

22

Scene of a hat
                    walking away.
Scene white with sun
                         until she is sitting on a wall
in a field
          where the sun breaks down
                                        because another sun
has come quietly in.

One of Varda's signature gestures was having people look directly
into the camera. It creates the illusion that no artifice stands
between us and these people who could be we.

We see
Agnès V.
          setting up a camera on a black and white street
          to take a photo of Brassai from several different heights

which is why she has dragged a ladder through the streets in the
rain along with a cumbersome, antique camera and its heavy glass
plates among all other odds, a man stands to be photographed
against an aging wall.

One of the things I'm particularly drawn to in Varda's work is the
way she so often presented landscape as accidental, incidental—
no big deal, inevitable—but then you gradually realize that it's the
very center and composed of openings
                              (the little door in the sun
that the film is based upon

something breaking—

the liquidity of light

in how many packages per second

interrupted by her face.

It's a gesture of pure rupture—the face of the filmer breaking open the surface of the fiction—though her work is often cast as documentary, it's the filmer's face here that forces us to recognize that even what's true is made.

Landscape in the shade

of oak over stream

Landscape of leaves

floating down the stream

Landscape of reflected clouds

that they reshuffle

Landscape of flowers leaning over

the clouds and the leaves

and not moving.

Though, actually, the word *filmer* doesn't seem to exist. One who films. Yes, but one who does so as a gesture of vision—in short, as a way of seeing and being

able to leave it at that.

Landscape of trees

planted equidistant

a forest organized

into mind

into pieces of time.

Landscape of rakes through gravel

       the rooms

thrown open as a matter of principle.

Landscape with light in panes

       across a piano, glasses empty

on a tray.

Varda moved smoothly from analogue into digital, but then realized that it made her film stock redundant, which she, in turn, recognized as a new raw material.

So she made it into houses. First, life-sized cabins in which she could literally live in film. And then miniature ones: out of the old stock of *Le Bonheur*, she made a cage filled with sunflowers. Of *La Pointe Courte*, she made a small boat in which they did not sail away in light. Instead, light filters through the literal materiality of the film, thus filtering through the faces of the filmed, which in turn, are projected onto the face of the person living within.

So something opens in space that one can hold.

         Begin with a stair

then a door

      Landscape of the window

just behind the door

      Landscape of the table

just below the window

      Landscape that opened

a window in the wall

      and now the ghosts are children

in front of everything green.

The panes repeat in light
that stains across the floor.

Landscape of feathers
                            that come and go across the woman, old.
The feathers are the snow
                      you held for years until it shut.

Varda said that her career spanned three distinct modes: first, photographs, then film, and then later, installation. Her 2009 work, *Bord de Mer*, for instance, brought the sea inside, a film and a photographic still working together across the gallery floor and wall, nothing but sand and sea and sky.

On a beach:
                  Two doves
are sitting on her chest
                in the sun, a third
tucked into the crook of her arm.

Landscape of yellow
                    once also sun, which has now
been forgotten and makes us forget
                        what was
that lovely fading something loved
                        for which
another day was made.

Toward the end of her second Norton lecture at Harvard in the Spring of 2018, Varda said, *This is about time; this is about time.* And it's true; we're trapped in it. You can glance at a painting, a photograph, a sculpture, an installation; you can even skim a written work, but you must give film its time; there's no way to rush it—like theater or performance, but with the difference of presence—we're used to live things, *presentations*, having a fixed, and determining, temporal dimension, but a representation that includes such rigid temporality is an anomaly—or a modernity— and is, in a certain sense, a contradiction, and the tension of that forms a taut surface, like that of a drum, both resonant and fragile.

Landscape with a more fragile landscape behind it. *If you give yourself time to sit here, time is part of the work.*

Landscape of boats and their lights
                                        Landscape of boats at night
Landscape of night on a table

Landscape of a table—
                        it's a banquet in honor of someone
just out of the frame to the right.

Zao Wou-ki
Enter Weather

In colored air   thought lit and sung   raw in all detail—

God is, as they say, there in detail—and everything here, elemental, immediate, emergence
                                        occurs second by second, the presence
of time in infinitesimal spaces.

Landscape with Crescent Moon: sliver as foundational principle sliding through.

Though after 1959, Zao Wou-Ki increasingly titled his paintings with the date on which he finished them, his earlier works often have strikingly evocative titles that underscore his strong ties to poets and to poetry. *Dust and wind*
                          between two cities
            after the eclipse
                          a village en fête

As a child he studied calligraphy, which may be what gives his works the feeling, not only of abstract landscapes, but also of abstract manuscripts, herds of signs flooding a distance that planes, that flies flat into the haunt of the hand as it makes its way across space. Migration has about it something always of the early, or maybe even something of the not quite born, perhaps it's simply an insistence that crosses waves and leaves, and even more—there were even more delicate things to list and arrange.

More trees dissolving into fields. When one emigrates, one is shorn, and the skin goes on, a transparent membrane that talks in its sleep. Zao Wou-Ki first visited Paris in 1948 and went immediately to the Louvre with its great windows looking out over the Seine
                    flight of birds over the river
in an exploding curve
finished in yellow. Could have been *27.08.82*, each cut of wing in its slice of sky, in its line of soft incising, the fact of flock. And at that point, he said, *my painting became illegible.*

Thus rendering it visible and collapsing time into a bright point radiating outward—*red maple*
                         a conflagration
                                   somewhere else

Zao was born into a family that traced its ancestry back to the 10th century Song dynasty. They had plates in the kitchen that been in the family for almost a thousand years. When he was a child, they held an annual viewing of the family treasures, which included a painting by the 11th century master, Mi Fu, who remained a compelling model for him throughout his life: *Above all a painter who saw differently, a great calligrapher*

brings the birds back
                                        to cut the sky into signs

It has been said (Tamon Miki, 1977) that the English word 'calligraphy' doesn't fully capture what is meant by *sho* in Japanese or *ch'u* in Chinese; the English word lacks the extent, the kinetic *geste* of the gesture, which is not limited to those already known, those gestures that inscribe a readily decipherable sign. The Japanese and Chinese terms also indicate an overflow, an orchestral sweep that pours into figuration, creating of association a literal field—language surpassing its own signification through the creation of territory.

As do the bone characters that show up in *Wind*, which some consider Zao's breakthrough work, all ink in the dark, charting a course through which this most ancient Chinese script suggests language as landscape itself. Which led him to collaborate with some of the greatest poets of his time—René Char, Saint-John Perse, Ezra Pound, Roger Laporte,
                                        and earlier ones: Rimbaud
Rimbaud, and Rimbaud
and always, in endless conversation, Henri Michaux.

It's through friendship that abstraction can acquire a density sufficient to amount to matter. To become material. And Michaux with his own calligraphic migrations across blank light, with his new alphabet in which the thousands silhouetted along the horizon become individual ideograms. They became fast friends.

And you can have, beyond the friend, beyond the person standing right in front of you, a friendship with a culture or aesthetic persuasion with which you have never had any contact whatsoever

in the *village en fête*

in *the red sun*

or wake up in the middle of the night speaking in tongues.

Paul Klee once woke up in the middle of the night, strongly influenced by both Chinese and Japanese art, scratching his signs in series that conflate the written page and the map. Perhaps it was that that so struck Zao—a map of light breaking form in half.

Zao's work itself as cartography and thus as a kind of crossing, and then there's the fact that his given name, Wou-Ki, means "no boundaries." We cross by dissolving form into motion, noun into verb, managing a slide from experience to expression, the hand never leaving the paper—he said, "I cannot

with a horse

crossing at such

and then the horse gave up

which is what it is

to become a sign, and the sign become a space that begins in the mind and comes to glaze a distance

into color that leaves

a light on inside—

for instance, *Untitled*, 1976 is alive and the animal lost inside is standing on the edge of a cliff, looking past.

32

Sally Mann
Untitled Ground

In every one of her photos, there's something you can't quite
see—some blind spot that's worked its way up from within.

For instance, *Bridge of Tallahatchie*, 1998, from the "Deep South"
series—what is it that's sitting in the upper branches off to the left,
a tangle of old children too late to be read

from a long way back, a depth of time ringing in the eye, often
under trees.

Back is a path they unravel, collecting shades—She said she was
trying to get them to give up their graves:

Battlefields, Manassas (Veins), 2000, along its horizon, there's
something large on fire a long way off; something we can't see
about history is burning up from the back of the gelatin silver print—

Battlefields, Antietam (Cornfield), 2001, move on, through the
sound, its famous kind of wind—dry stalks, brittle sun, the long

leaves of the dead plants, like a paper cut, shut

the history of the south, keep your hands out, out of the fire, keep them out of the light, or they'll burn in, permanent, all over the face of them—

Battlefields, Cold Harbor (Battle), 2003, how silently the trees retreat while their leaves explode; it's the cold we know, it's the harbor we don't—drop your hand down into the water and watch it flinch.

The sanctity of this death-inflected soil
                                    within every inch, its names
untied these hundreds of years
                        of the rhythm of its work
working whose blood back down into its heart.

How odd that a tree can be shot and it doesn't even seem to hurt. Odd that, in this photo, through a simple accident of emulsion, bullets still seem to be wind that just happen to all be heading to the right in shreds. But much odder still is how far back you can go, perpendicular to those bullets' paths, farther and farther, fields flying low, she walks out of the back of the photograph undoing and undone, keep on unraveling a tomb, said comb it through, and where did that voice suddenly come from—

if it's not, in fact, her own: *I am reminded of the powdery bones shifting uneasily beneath all of it.* And yet, despite all that, had to say that she felt at home. And so took a photograph:

Battlefields, Antietam (Trenches), 2001, in which there's a flaw in the emulsion almost exactly in the middle of the composition, so brightly white that, again, it can only come from inside. While all the rest of the light has been caught in a net, flecks that help you forget—and who said, *it's not that you forgot that matters, but that you forgot that you did.*

She studied photography in a number of places—1971, at a film school in Denmark and at a fine arts school in Greece, and then, 1973, at the Apeiron Workshop and the Ansel Adams Yosemite Workshop, quoting Minor White: *to invoke the invisible within the visible.* In each of her works, there's a blind spot, and it saves us

from ever letting the photograph settle down to a single, finished thing; instead it's a two-dimensional surface that never stops becoming what it will never be.

Alexander Gardner, *Antietam, Bodies of Confederate Dead Gathered for Burial*, 1862. There were so many scattered across the field that you could have walked it diagonally without touching ground.

Who there had sown the death within
                                    these very men
among their broken hands. Bones build a land. To turn your back on. The turned back of time.

Death, the precipitate of a supersaturated history; begin at the beginning:
          The first enslaved people to arrive on the North American continent landed in 1619 at Point Comfort, Virginia, only one year

after "the Great Charter" had given the evolving Virginia Company the beginnings of representative government. A promise still thwarted, as late as 1966, by the Virginia poll tax. Sally Mann's mother, in addition to chairing the Lexington Interracial Committee and founding the local League of Women Voters, was among those who worked tirelessly to overturn it.

It, another kind of battlefield with its own kind of darkness enveloping it, the sort that you can't get to show up in a photograph. In which everyone who ever passed stumbled on exactly the same stone
      and broke a wrist
which shifted chance—
      an accident of history
for centuries.
If you see it in slow-enough motion, it's all the work she's ever done walking out of the picture like someone who had a choice.

Mann got her first camera, an old Leica, in 1969; it had been her father's, and though he was from Texas and her mother from Boston, Mann herself is from the South, and took it like an oath. And felt it in her chest, that stone

kept the stone in grief, from hand to hand, and passed it back again. *Men, Janssen*, 2006-2015, the fingers of the hands are interlaced across the dark chest, a patterned braid of bony flesh against which the nails stand out, bright—unnaturally so—they practically glow, and, in fact, you ask, what is it exactly that's happening at the ends of those hands?

And so the war rages on: *Battlefields, Antietam (Starry Night)*, 2001, the stars scarring across both the dark field and the dark sky; only the trees are alive, and they live only on light. The black and white is somehow accurate, somehow permanent—

Battlefields, Antietam (Black Sun), 2001, with nothing distinguishable across the entire field of mottled grey until the horizon suddenly cuts, precisely delineating the fine detail of a farm cart, a hay rick, a bare tree, impossibly, as our eyes adjust, we begin to see a rail fence running at an angle, but not sharply enough to ever reach us.

Us: there's an element of witness requested, maybe even demanded, that makes one aware that *yes, I have seen this*

is the contract inherent in all photography, which is therefore inherently a declaration of its and our participation in the polity.

Sally Mann's extensive work photographing Civil War battlefields, bringing out their indelible darkness, is also a staging of an internal battle between her personal history and its public ramifications. As an upper-middle class white person, with all the privilege that that entails, raised in part by a black woman who left her own family every morning to take care of theirs, she had a moment of shock and recoil when, as a teenager, she saw her various worlds suddenly from a larger social perspective, and found herself reeling from a recognition of her unwitting responsibility and complicity.

Yes, I have seen this photograph as an act of defiance against a personal past that stretches back into an injury inflicted over centuries and by centuries man-handling the word *own*. And so I must. Own it. And my own shadow pitched therein.

She described it as *awakening from a fathomless sleep of ignorance*. In the chapter of her autobiography titled "Who Wants to Talk About Slavery?" she stated simply *I am doing my best to visually articulate my sense of the unsettled accounts left to us by the brooding curse*. Which necessitates a return to the battle still rooted in the ground it was fought upon.

Though the Battle of Antietam remains the deadliest day in United States history, it was that victory that gave Lincoln the political momentum he needed to issue the Emancipation Proclamation, which he did five days later. And while that document did not, in itself, completely abolish slavery, it was an essential step toward that goal.

Mann's work raises the issue of the connection between landscape and history, but also and more pointedly that between landscape and memory—does the earth remember grief? And what happens to grief when the griever looks up from the earth, raises their eyes; what happens to the sky? And what does that do to distance? Does it extend it? And by that extension, do we not share with it a mind? Or, rather, is distance itself a mind in which grief invites us to participate? And its relationship to time? All that cannot move through space glides through time, at times with grace, at times with grief, which we hear in an ear buried deep.

The *Blackwater* series, 2008-2012: All blasted by something that raged past, which was perhaps simply the past itself, *trying to reconcile my love for this place and its brutal history*. And yet she's said she feels that photographs actually rob us of the past by subtly, insidiously, replacing our memories with themselves.

When Mann photographed Antietam, she did so with the technology and materials available at the time of the battle—an 8 x 10 view camera and a wet-plate collodion process.

Battlefields, Antietam (Last Light), 2001, the entire thing is a ghost; she worked the wet plate until it lived with the dead living from within, the process taking force, taking the form rising from the ground unseen. Can using an obsolete process pull out of the past all that we missed, all that walked on by, gun in hand, an ambiguous man off to the right. We didn't see him at the time, the light didn't last, and that is not what is trapped at the far back of the photo among what you loved among trees.

So, first: clean the glass plate.

in which she sees her own face, leaning over in a circular motion

then melt potassium iodide and cadmium bromide in water, add to collodion; pour slowly and evenly across the glass; bring the whole thing to a shiver

　　　　　　in which we see her, black cloth over her head and shoulders, part of the camera's architecture, and quickly

into a bath of silver nitrate in the dark the sensitized hands take the plate out, place it into the negative carrier, and then the carrier into the camera over which she leans and into and maybe she just stays there, just looking. There's something in it, after all, if staying is to stain, or if to stray, in some deep way, you must

Fix the plate in sodium thiosulfate—fix there the error that will make it—that something tearing back across the field in streaks,

a field wrong in ardor, to capture the error that we all are— something in the lens remembers its forgetting as someone stumbling through a forest with his hands outstretched. He didn't live—none of them did—leaving aside the instructions, pouring lavishly the emulsion, refusing to polish the glass to perfection, which lets it strike back, pock, and pierce.

Battlefields: Manassas (Airplane): a great tree looming up on the low horizon in the dark a tree is as large as anything can or ever will be, and fire rains down the sky.

In all these photos, it's the damage—that's the thing that's really at work—the destruction of surface and its consequent insistence— the defiance of something as fragile as paper, as ephemeral as light, both equally torn apart, and a single streak, more like a cut, refracts off the back (*Antietam, Smoke*) Antietam ghost, Antietam as the palm of a hand sliced or rather flayed Antietam bone Antietam shone past and then beyond

Deep South, Untitled (Scarred Tree), 1998.

Chaïm Soutine
Reeling Trees

The children are lost—is the central fact—and that—
is what holds on—what factors in

and what losing is—how its moving parts
come together with that clicking sound—how are

we a product of wind? Everything here is

four paintings by Chaïm Soutine
hanging in a single room—though of only

two scenes—two of large trees—and two of
two children running home—we see them at two

different points on their road where
the capacious sky backs up—fills with trees—huge

trees full of wind that we can see—warm wind along

the road that behind them curves
beyond the curve where a world—which he built—from paint

painted over paint—breaks
into a world just barely—out of sight

it opens out—into a broad valley—dotted with majestic oaks
alone—in great fields of horses in a storm—the children are on—

their way home. Clarisse Nicoïdski said that
Soutine is the painter who made the wind visible—

In the curve of a feeling, as he put it, feeling always curves sharply toward, having been raised in a tradition that prohibited representation, he chose self-exile, arriving in Paris in 1913 (though some sources say 1912) at the age of 20, or perhaps 19 or 21, having had the liberty of not knowing quite when he was born

and went to stay with friends at La Ruche, with its affordable studio-housing built from the ruins of the most recent Universal Exhibition. Soutine was a great reader of Montaigne who claimed that the world is constantly churning, never achieving equilibrium. And so Soutine's riotous slippages multiply, and the viewer, too, slips, skids, and the trees reel overhead.

Landscape with Person or *The White Road*, 1918-1919
We're falling up a hill—still as the light shines through—
climbing branches that hold a house up to the sky

as the road divides—as the cliff falls—
as the sky falls—and the road flays

and the world tilts red where it isn't
walking along a road thrown farther up

as we pick our way down the red cliff
running in the sun.

Or   more   slowly—wandering   under   light—sharpening—the
light—making color—come off on the hands—and—sometimes
the hands—are larger than life and—always the hands—living on
their own

"… waiting for the wind to rise," he said to a friend who, passing
again hours later, found him sitting in exactly the same position.

And then it did:
Landscape Near Céret, 1920
if the house entered the wind—or rather
if the wind is—in fact—or becomes—the windows

or in what order—wind and house arrange
themselves—there is a shroud

to find—or lace or veil at times—the whole town
wearing out, wearing down—to the face

of the animal beginning to show through
the procession of white walking out of itself—not

as violent as one would have thought or
it was not the wind.

Soutine painted some 200 landscapes around Céret in the three years he spent there between 1919 and 1922. His first dealer, Zborowski, took him down to the south to give him the time and means to paint. First to Cagnes, just west of Nice, but Soutine was restless, and so moved on to Céret, a small town just above the Spanish border, some 20 miles from the sea. Dr. Albert Barnes, who put the entire Paris art world into a frenzy when he came in 1923 to buy contemporary works to fill his new foundation, encountered Soutine's work and was instantly struck, making a permanent and positive change in the latter's fortunes.

Barnes ended up acquiring 60 of the Céret landscapes, though another source puts the number at 100. Many others, Soutine cut up or burned in anxious fits in which he couldn't stand his own work.

He went through these fits off and on all his life. His good friend Paulette Jourdain once, hearing strange sounds from within, looked through the keyhole into his room and saw him in a rage, slashing canvases and ripping them to shreds. He once commented to another painter, *One day, I'm going to assassinate my paintings*.

Zborowski routinely fished them out of the garbage and gallerists refused to sell his works back to him, knowing what he'd do to them. At other times he would stare at a painting for a while, then go over to it, cut out a particular part, and keep just that.

Many of the landscapes are towns, and many others are trees. For instance, *The Oak*, c. 1939, which is mostly sun, and *The Tree* c. 1939 with houses the size of marbles somewhere down below. Is a painting of a tree a landscape or a portrait? He painted so aggressively that one day he dislocated his thumb.

—

The Old Mill, 1922-1923
For someone loved a forest—and someone loved the trees
on the side of a hill falling home—another home

and their curving green—we always seem
to be drifting back—back past the paint where the world

looks just like this—and because an object is
as it is loved—a road, a house, a sun—it comes

to join—the trees in their unlikely light.

If you consider the height of the sky, take it as a gauge and how distance aligns with distortion, the slant of horizon, and the chaos that is always about to turn into abstract expressionism.

Avenue of Trees, 1936
There's an important unspoken unshaken ratio
between tree and human always at work

in which trees rise unbearably—searingly—trees in all their
monumentality arching over protectively—the line of trees

forms a single intelligent animal—holding the tiny people in fragile thrall—a road lined with trees—is irresistible—

and uncannily—a door. Uncanny because you knew it would be there, and that its frame would be painted red.

Soutine hated to be watched at work, and in fact would refuse to paint in the presence of anyone else. He once put a foot through a piece he was working on because someone stopped and looked over his shoulder. And he was known for grabbing his canvas and clutching it to his chest if he saw someone coming. You can imagine. According to his chauffeur, the reason he painted so many versions of the giant ash tree in Vence was that there was a niche nearby in which he could hide, certain of not being observed. But just to be sure, he posted the chauffeur right outside to discourage any curious passers-by. *That tree*, he said, *is a cathedral*. And the chauffeur replied *I'd rather have a horrid Soutine than a masterpiece by anyone else*.

Arbre de Vence c. 1929: tree that *errance* be: *principe*: that tree in sky *déplie*, an *eventail* fanned out against a town an error away. Legend claims that the tree was planted by François Premier.

—

And the trees bring us back to the children of which there are several in motion. *Two Children on a Road*, 1942, Museum of Art and History, Geneva. Who, at the front edge of the frame, anchor the hill that billows up behind them and up the sky. *Two Children on a Road*, 1939, Israel Brener Collection, Mexico City. This time

they're looking at each other in the middle of a track of yellow sand
between green fields, again, a small hill, it's almost a little dance;
they can't be older than five or six beneath the same sky as it's
forced out of the picture by everything rising in sight.

The children are lost—is the central fact—and that—
is what inheres—what shares the act

that losing is—and how it loosens
the ties that hold their bodies in—how we

are just a whim. Everything here is
children turned to wind—is air shearing

the light off the skin. They ran
because they loved the storm they were running in.

In 2006, a film was made on Soutine that includes interviews
done in the 1960s with people who had known him. One woman
mentions that her mother was a nurse in Civry, where Soutine and
Garda lived in 1939, and that, as a child, she would accompany
her mother when she went to treat him for his stomach malady. *I
would go with her sometimes. Soutine was always very kind to
me. The two children in the road are my cousin and I.*

Two Children Sitting on a Log, 1942-43, private collection. They
are sitting down because the road behind them is long. They are
older now, with sharper features, and by that time, he was living
in Champigny-sur-Veude with Marie-Berthe Aurenche. And it goes
on like that until his death a year later—the open space, the space

of the picture-plane opening up at the back, falling out   with the trees still straining up. *Two Children at Champigny Beneath a Blue Sky*, c. 1943, private collection. It's true, though there is only one, running straight on. Throughout his work there's often a confusion or conflation of children, trees, and houses, as if they were all equally places that we live.

Joan Jonas
Merlo, 1974

Here, too the landscape is almost entirely wind   a woman
veiled head to toe   in a dark cloth   standing on a balustrade

in Tuscany, grainy   black and white video   from the mid-1970s
the veil constantly rearranged   by the wind silhouetting

the body into mercury. She was the first artist to use live video in
her work, sometimes paralleling her performances with live feed

filtering into mercury   into the trees   into a migration   amid
displacements   profiled against drift   which makes it into

a pilgrimage, patches of mist   rising in the valley behind her.
Her body is often at the center of her work, but it's never
autobiographical   so she's invulnerable.   Patches of mist

are somehow essential to the blackbird at the heart of the piece.

merlo, merlo

At the heart of the emerging genre of performance art in New York at the end of the 1960s, she saw a link between that and the equally emergent women's movement.   The woman is tall

across the broad valley   across the dark field   with the dirt road running off under trees   full of blackbirds   full in darkness somewhere farther back there   her stepfather was an amateur

magician and so as a child, she fell in love with sleight of hand, the slight *and*   that sees no end   under the trees full though in fact   though birds appear throughout her work

here there's no bird in sight   though dogs bark, drawing the evening out   into a dark that carves   into things that slip   from thing to hand to chance.   *I didn't see a major*

difference between a poem, a sculpture, a film, or a dance. Sometimes the birds are simply drawn.   Sometimes they remain alone.   She often draws without looking at the paper

keeping her eyes instead on the model   somewhere farther the barking dogs out of sight to the left   are haunting an echo that creates a third dimension   within the screen   the barking

continues to make its own rhythm inherently a part of the night. *I used to work only at night.* "Did the sound carry over the water?"

We know that a river   runs down there   at the bottom of the valley   a strip of darkness   moving swiftly through hills

merlo, merlo
black among its wing

Among the animals throughout her work   moving swiftly through
mythology and fairy-tale   every animal is   in fact its own

myth, hauling centuries along inside it.   And every dog is, in fact
also a path. And the barking, a gong   as a crowd   as a shroud

hidden in wind. She drew her own dog so often that he finally
came in.   Ritual, choreography, and mirroring are elements that

she has insistently foregrounded throughout the last fifty years—
and then, there's the wind—a ritualistic choreography of mirrors

in its own right   and how the wind turns to night   by making
the road its own   in the lone road   that the woman on

the balustrade watches run. It was not there before.   It's the
barking of the dogs that we call home. *Wind*, 1968—her first film

and her first work made outdoors; wind whips across a beach on
Long Island covered in snow.   Wind further makes the river

flying over   the bird in black   backed up against a landscape
that must once have been in color.   Juxtaposition also plays a

central role in her compositions, the dramatic shift creating a rift
through which new animals slip.   Patches of mist rising up to

find them. When seen, the dogs are white, but this is years later
and they are heading off somewhere else   which is, for them,

a precise location. Herding all waters, herding all verges, a pastoral
economy depends upon affection   to ensure the safety

of its everything wandering. If a woman for instance walks across
a river, if a road follows her, if bird and dog become increasingly

a part   if we see ourselves as also inextricable   would we reach
for the bird or for the dog?   The barking becomes a vehicle

carrying us farther and farther into the background. She works
as much outside as in, avoiding the word *nature* and replacing it
with that of distance.   And the dogs barking within it.

And barking, again,   it's Tuscany in spring   the bells turned
inside-out watch a woman on a stone railing, carefully   a river

at the bottom of a valley   finds itself   a bird on a balustrade.
The sound of the outdoors   I consider how sound is delayed.

A woman is calling across a river.   She is waiting for an answer.
How is a bird distilled to thin air?   And in what other forms

will the dogs appear? We stay out late on the terrace overlooking
the valley—   late enough that the mist   has taken on a life

a background for rifer birds   lined up   along a balustrade   a
simple   stone construction   on which one might lean

an elbow   or pose a fan   folded   to fool the wind.

Henry Ossawa Tanner
Night Over Night

We're considering only the late works because it's only in them
that night gets built of light, letting contradiction lock into place as
the principal engine of Tanner's oeuvre. It is a contradiction that he
had lived all his life, an active disruption of the distinction between
dark and light, between black and white.

Night, in which things become unfixed, unlimned: his later
paintings—something flies apart in them as something flies within

Tanner, a quiet man, for whom painting a landscape was a mode
of displacement, a form of travel, not only from one place to
another, but from self to self, one hand on the handle of a door.
You paint the handle, and then you open the door. *Le Touquet*,

c. 1910, on the Normandy coast, near their house in Trópicd in
the moon in the clouds over the azure is such an ocean heralding
form. Two people are heading home beneath two trees that are
still there, now leaning over two other people, protecting them.

Tanner became a leader of the artists' community centered in the nearby fishing village of Étaples. International in nature, it started in the early 1880s and thrived until 1914, but never quite recovered from the war.

Tanner, however, continued to live there, with his wife and son and best friends, Atherton and Ingeborg Curtis. When his wife died in 1925, he moved to a different house, internalizing the shroud, and continued to live there until almost the end of his life, which he spent more or less rewriting the Bible from the perspective of night—a sweep and a glimpse feathered in shade,

a wraith of blue with a corner of the night sky in its eye   dotted with streetlights or with torches held up, allowing the sharp leap into sight to continue moving forward, drawing the painting along in its wake   *The disciples*   *The foolish virgins*   The center of a life in which night shows us just how everything living is lit from within. And given that painting is all about seeing, the decision to focus on the very point at which seeing breaks down, breaks out into other senses, puts pressure on intuition, on reflection, on invention, and on every other way by which we see.

Tanner first left the United States in 1891, on his way to Rome via London and Paris, but once in Paris, he simply didn't move on, but instead started classes at the Académie Julian. Tanner: *Strange that after having been in Paris a week, I should find conditions so to my liking that I completely forgot when I left New York I had made my plans to study in Rome and was really on my way there . . .*

But let's go back to the night, and via the proposition that, for Tanner, painting offered a vehicle for overflowing circumstances and context, for flowing out of the United States, thereby eroding the boundaries of nation, self, and personal history by focusing

on the night, which is inherently borderless—within it, things have no edges, things live indeterminate; less themselves alone, they begin to participate in others; they start suggesting and transforming—in evening is the transformation of the world— Tanner made a particular study of twilight because in it the seen and the unseen strike a perfect balance, and in it light has more layers than at any other hour.

In the summer of 1891, he found himself in the artists' colony of Pont Aven, made known by Sérusier, Bernard, and Gauguin. 1892, summer again, and another spot in Brittany, Concarneau. And then, 1897, a trip to "the Holy Land" sponsored by a patron who thought Tanner needed to see the actual sites of his scenes.

Once there, however, he painted what he saw: *A Mosque in Cairo, The Jews' Wailing Place, A View of Palestine* stretching out past tree-lined ravines to an iridescent sky, his interest in religion seeming to embrace them all evenly. And often through architecture—the mosque, the wall, the architecture of faith picked out in right angles by the architecture of light.

He also continued painting biblical scenes: *Nicodemus*, 1899, who will, much later, bring the spices for the embalming, now sitting on a terrace across from a young Jesus behind whom the city is not so much a matter of buildings as it is of the density and tangibility of evening turning air into powdered cobalt, a material that became a center of Tanner's research, becoming a land in itself, in which increasingly he lived, sieved into vivid prescience.

He did another version much later, 1927; this time they're sitting on a rooftop, and the night has gotten bluer. There's a small pile of it in the hand that Jesus holds out, as if weighing it against what he'll say next.

The 1897 trip solidified the crucial role of travel in Tanner's life. Perhaps having grown up as an outsider, he was tempted to keep on going, getting more and more outside, seeing how far it would go until it ultimately crystalized into a total inclusivity, as every bit of territory that you cross, once behind you, becomes internalized. And so, the farther you go, the larger the inside grows, until, in fact, it's all within; it's just a matter of time.

His travels also sent him back to the biblical stories on which he'd been raised, though going back physically made it apparent that any return is also entering new territory. The son of a bishop in the African Methodist Episcopalian Church, Tanner was a committed believer, though at some point, he seems to have exchanged the church for the quiet night to convey the unexplained in a pencil drawing of the unsaid in the margin of a small carnet—

> "this is what you missed
> that now so misses you."

And practically speaking, biblical themes were very popular and sold quite well at the end of the 19th century, fluidly fusing with the

Symbolist spirit as well as with that of the Nabis and various other post-impressionist movements. And so he continued to paint them: *The Good Shepherd*, 1902-03, beneath the moon and two great oaks while off to the right, distance accrues a ridge behind which the void begins in a rush of azure.

The oak, too, comes back: *Abraham's Oak*, 1905, in smoke grey of the great age of the full moon of an endless tree (Isaiah 61:3) (In 1852, a bolt of lightning struck off a branch, and it took eight camels to haul off the wood.) And yet a small house, white and well in the distance, persists. And persists in difference, as white as its moon—a square against a circle, alight, and so thrives.

Difference was a theme always present for Tanner, though not often dramatized, more likely just suggested, at times through a stylistic focus on indeterminacy. Indeterminacy radicalizes difference by making everything suddenly different from itself, by disrupting the stability that anchors a base line from which things are or are not different. Instead, we see all elements in relative motion, with each creating the others and being created by them, paradoxically both making them all more distinct and erasing all apparent boundaries between them as they fuse into an intricate system. Another of the contradictions that drove him, and drove him toward shadows; shadows make us listen acutely and heighten the tactile attention that lies in a thin layer

all over the skin, kinetically within: shadow-heft, the lilting time of time cast back and the backward time of blue. The century turned, and Tanner developed a new palate in which usually cool colors, again from within, turned warm—greens and steels in the heat of the moon, whose light is made of mica, thinly layered and ricocheting within.

Tanner spent years perfecting his glazes, refining his recipes, balancing fragility and clarity, the delicate snap of anything transparent, even in the evening, through which his figures walk lightly, almost shell becoming dust beneath their way. He laid glaze upon glaze until they were looking down through ice suspended, in which, as if the trite metaphor of time as a river had suddenly frozen over, there hovered a face turning away to walk back down the road to Bethany (oil on canvas, 1902-03, Musée d'Orsay) with two others who have already turned completely into that earlier era, which has, in turn, turned warm again, a summer night outlined in moon.

Atherton to Tanner in a letter from the early 1930s:
                                                    I hope there
was some blue or green paint among those you unpacked. It would be a pity if you had to substitute red for blue and paint sunsets or things on fire instead of moonlight.

Moonlight, Walls of Tangier, 1913, a luminous grey washing the sky across the face of a building. His first two trips to North Africa, 1908 & 1910, soaking his purples in the sun. The North Africa paintings include the only later works outside in broad daylight, even drenched in it, light running down the walls and doorways and arches. We are looking through an Arabic portal, and the light pouring through makes a halo of the head of the back-lit figure walking in.

This, of course, simply records the reality of the place, but perhaps it's also a metaphor for the relative lightness that he felt upon finding himself for the first time in a society not dominated by white Europeans and their descendants, even though the issue of race had largely ceased to be a limiting factor in his life once he'd moved to France.

And though not completely free of the French colonial gaze, he avoided its clichés and depicted North African cities and people in an unusual light—calm, frank, and vibrant all at once.

> And twice: Light as a narrative element.
> Light saying if and what if, and then when

light is a story in itself—in fact, light as the only story—Eakins (paraphrased): "light as the principal tool" building buildings: *Entrance to the Casbah*, 1912, a shimmering mirage of yellow rushing forth against a donkey moving slowly in the heat that now warms the room in Lafayette, Indiana where the painting currently hangs.

    Gateway, Tangier, 1910, again, we are led always more inside. And, as always with his work, we also go inside the night—

    Algiers, Old Buildings Near Ka-hak, 1912, up on a hill where a moon we can't see gilds the vanilla buildings in mercury. Or *Palace of Justice, Tangier*, 1912-13, which is actually a flight into Egypt; the Holy Family, having by now been flying for almost two thousand years, walks peacefully through the public square, late in opal, hoping never to get there.

These works mark the end of a transition he'd been making since the early 1900s toward an atmospheric cerulean based on transparencies applied serially in sheets over a bright white ground, the white increasingly covered over, through which it increasingly shone. He worked, too, in a strangely serial manner;

because each application of glaze took a while to dry, he worked on ten or twenty paintings at a time which must have made him feel like he was wandering throughout the entire Bible, passing through the Annunciation, the Visitation, the Last Supper, and so on, like they were rooms in a mansion of which they were also the windows.

Unlike others of his era who were experimenting with form and abstraction, Tanner focused his experiments on the materials themselves, seeing in the visceral matter of his medium a vitality and necessity that wouldn't be taken up again until the middle of the century. His experiments addressed the gaze as diffused by certain preparations of paint that let the glaze gaze back— up to 21 layers

of fishermen coming home through the night, now slightly green in transparent chromium viridian, adorned with warm lantern, requiring a hand attached to a tired man attached to a tired son trudging uphill behind him.

Let's stop a moment at the lantern—It became a recurrent character, and often associated with the inhabitants of Étaples— *Return at Night from the Market* (1912), *Étaples Fisher Folk* (1923), *The Fisherman's Return* (1926)—stark against the dark, an errant shard of sun held in and held in a hand or placed on the ground within reach.

For a Christian, the issue of fish, fishing, and fishermen cannot *not* have multiple densely impacted meanings (*The Miraculous Haul of Fishes*, 1913-14), and the fact that fishermen often work at night, bringing a light home with them, the fact that a lantern is itself a small house made wholly of windows from which a light looks out alone.

This offers a good illustration of one of Tanner's guiding principles: he located the light inside of things, which is easier to find at night, and brought it to the surface, where it glowed and then overflowed. This is the physiology of the halo.

His 1935 glaze recipe: best linseed soaked, raw or lightly cooked, then the glue: soak goat parchment 24 hours, simmer, but do not boil. Add oil, linseed or poppy, to mastic varnish. Dissolve lanoline in mineral essence. Add 90% alcohol—it will emulsify better. Mix it all together until it attains the consistency of butter.

63

Agnes Martin
Homage to Untitled Life

They are points. They float and dive. They point alive. They epitomize the inviolable nobility of the intransitive verb. They point into time.

These points are placed in the spaces formed by the grids drawn on three 9 x 9 ink, pencil, and/or gauche drawings in room #9.

Drawing as the language of the line. The line as the language of space. (*A line begins as a point in space.*) A line constitutes one of the clearest and most comprehensive forms of measure because it measures the space it crosses as it also creates it, unfolds it, and always unfolding farther, the line is timed to the pulse of its lateral falling, unwinding its patience from inside.

Drawing begins in graphite, with its mineral glint, its granular and crumbling light, anthracite within. There is something about graphite that is relentlessly internal, always an inner eye. *Acrylic and graphite on canvas*, 2000. Glint that hovers, glint that glides, that the light of its darkness defies.

She would have denied this, seeing all art invariably in the positive.
(*… since all of life is positive.*)

Which is proved as light arrives   and is returned, sharper,
cut
        into a miracle of pencil
                                seemed so simple
                                        Lead on linen

as if any grey always had it halfway silvered   mirror-tarnished
half the line while the other half, the darker back, aligned, grave.

She later turned to paint, to rulers, to masking tape in the break
in the split
                second in which
                                the hand breaks down
which breaks out, which overflows, which ink will, or ink in water
in a wash   washes over   a fluid *and*.

And there are waves on the shore she said pointing to a washboard
of clouds in the sky, *my work has nothing to do with landscape*,
she said, several times, though never in response to anyone's
suggestion that it did. A landscape of clouds in a wallpaper pattern
that hauls the sky behind.

She was known for going for long drives. Sometimes she'd say to
a friend "Let's go for a drive." And hours later, sometimes days.
Distance is farther inside.

Martin was also a writer—the shadow of a hand floating over paper—
and her titles, which are other lines, equally fine, equally precise,
collapsing the distinction between the drawn and the written.

a sister night
by the sea stone
a falling sign
in flowered rain
wind in the blue
of friendship, night
in the sea of friends

how the simple builds
into grandeur simply
by the repetition of patience

burning wave
the tree In song
the song in field
falling white, little held
or the light that falls

was always yours
and is yours again
falling in a word

The writings that she conceived and intended as such—those
collected in *Writings*, for instance—are startlingly simple,
aphoristic, almost platitudes—*Beauty is the mystery of life*; *The
goal of life is happiness*; *Artwork is very valuable*—yet somehow,

against all odds, they amount to something very moving, sincere, and, ultimately, utterly convincing. Again, through repetition— beauty, happiness, the process of life. Is yours again.

Take, for instance, *The Islands*, 1961. Dating from her time at Coenties Slip and her carefully dovetailed reconciliation of a Calvinist background with Taoist-Zen sensibilities developed in conversations with Ad Reinhardt in the 1950s. A grid composed of 1,536 squares, each one dotted with four pale marks resembling dashes in Morse code. Specifically those that make the letter T. 6,144 of them. A sea.

In his essay for the 2015 Tate catalogue, Richard Tobin uses the term "vast" to talk about this painting—"a haze of vast ocean in deep *crepuscolo.*" That vast belongs to most, that vast an ocean chose the square.

On a single day, that single choice changed her entire body of work. The square inherently refuses hierarchy in its equal extension in all directions. And therefore functions sheerly as space.

Which eliminates the possibility of horizon, and so, for the first time, is able to depict the endlessness of the spherical, and so for the first time, a landscape not limited by an eye.

A waterfall, she said, anyone *can stand all day in front of a waterfall,* which hauls the land within. A falling night with wind.

And the shadow of its kind. There's shadow on the brain. Or perhaps it didn't seem like a shadow at all. She would ask a friend to go out for a drive.

She began using the grid in the early 1960s, and by 1963, it was her predominant form, suggesting weaving, a way of interlacing lines that fused time and space. She has often said that she was thinking of the innocence of trees.

Take, for instance, *The Tree*, 1964, staggering, forward and back. *Innocence,* she said, and there it was—a fact fracturing light.

If her grid is based in trees seen from far above, counting again under the breath, the bird's eye view is also a pacing step. And what would then be innocence? And what its relation to the intimate?

Martin, who repeatedly stated that *personal emotions . . . are anti-art*, made a neat distinction in her work, imbuing it with an intimacy entirely free of the personal, even of personality. Achieved by infusing the intimate with distance. As also has all innocence. You stand back a bit, utterly changed, before you the picture. And so she changed her life.

In 1967, Martin suddenly stopped painting, the hand poised mid-air, staying there, giving all her brushes and pigments away. She moved to Cuba, New Mexico, cut off from everything whenever it rained. Without plumbing or electricity, building her houses by hand.

And it rained again, a raging, flailing screen, straight down, staring out the window, wondering why a downpour, composed as it is of chains of transparent water, appears to the human eye as grey. As veiling a face thriving behind a sheet of sun.   She began painting again in 1975. Works often composed solely of horizontal lines. How might isolation be its own horizon. Or the vertical is the portrait, and now all the people are gone. And yet friendship remains. They'd go out for a drive or for days   she worked steadily up to her death almost thirty years later. The titles of some of her last works include *Homage to Life* and *The Sea*.

70

Robert Smithson
Mirrors & Their Placements

When you cut the sun, you cut the sky, and then it can be moved
in its smaller pieces; it's moving now because we are speaking,
with the sky behind our voices, the sky angled to take no notice,
the sky feigning, feinting; he took a very sharp knife and, entirely
freehand, cut the sky perfectly in half.

Mirror-shift

through broken light.   The sky, by definition, is never seen entire

and travels right along with us in a herd of fragments. 1969: Robert
Smithson, Nancy Holt, and Virginia Dwan made a trip through the
Yucatán   in the course of which   at nine locations   Smithson
placed twelve mirrors, each a foot square, at various angles in
various materials, disrupting everything around them.

First displacement: on the other side of the horizon between
Umán and Muná, in a place where the land is routinely cleared
by burning. In the surrounding ash, the mirrors are embedded
in a photograph of carbon dust retreating back into the forest.

In the mirrors, all we see are fissures and feathers, trees becoming finer and finer. A mirror always demands that you look more closely. The trees will not stop. It is morning, and there is light all over the ground, white as salt.

Smithson took the title of his essay "Incidents of Mirror-Travel in the Yucatan" from John L. Stephens' 1843 book *Incidents of Travel in Yucatan*. Stephens, an American writer, traveled extensively in the region from 1839 to 1842 with the English artist and architect Frederick Catherwood.

Stephens claimed to have been shocked by the Mayans' lack of interest in their people's ancient artworks. Many of the artifacts that Stephens and Catherwood collected ended up in the American Museum of Natural History, where Robert Smithson first saw them. The mirrors were made to sew these eras together again, which is the nature of a mirror—to never stop traveling backward.

The white salt   is a halt in the sun   the sun that far south in its granular ire. They were traveling in a car with a tourist guide open on the seat beside them, open to a map, and on the map in capital letters: UY U TAN A KIN PECH—*just hear the way they talk!* said one Mayan to another upon her first contact with a Spaniard.

YU CA TAN, 1517, the white salt in the eye of the sun, ground into and then out of the face traced on a block of limestone by the side of the road.

Second displacement: outside of Uxmal edging on cliffs, and as in the first, there's a curious use of the passive—here *the second displacement was deployed*—a key aspect of the displacements is a strange offset of agency—a grammatical displacement reinforces the physical one, allowing the elements of the world to be rearranged with no one's actually having had a hand in it. And further along they found a quarry and its limestone, which is itself a quarry, where, in its home, it's hunted down.

According to at least one source, both meanings of the word—a site where stone is mined and the victim of a hunt—have roots in the Latin *cor,* which means *heart,* and there it is: the heart, in freefall in the photograph, posing as a sky, diving into the heart of the earth with a violence that's practically electric, wrenching it open. The result is a map that builds up on your hands, on all hands, and creates even more hands to contain it.

There was a smaller cliff; there was limestone mixed, and the clouds fixed into a matrix of other geological materials—silica and silvering as a mode of answering, as if an echo among hills could be heard within even more hands folding in.

Third displacement: near Bolonchén de Rejón: Driving there, they drove through clouds of butterflies turning piles of rubbled lime into a swarm of flickered stone.

They tucked the mirrors in sand, and the swallowtails imprinted themselves thereon, their wingdust eroding their highly polished surfaces; *They seemed to fly through a sky of gravel.*

Always available and timeless   said Smithson   of mirrors but he was wrong—they're blinding clocks in the brilliant sun, making every grain of dust, including every face, account for every second of itself.

An Aztec god once used obsidian mirrors to tell the future while the Olmec used mirrors of hematite to light ritual fires.

Fourth displacement: Leaving Campeche, south along the Gulf coast, where the water is made of jade; we find the mirrors walking back up the beach, full of the sea and its foam, colored in now with the sea all broken down. You could pick up and hold a perfect square foot of it perfectly out of place. *Tidepools of sky,* they were on their way to Champoton full of an eden that refused all reason. They traveled with the windows down and the rear-view mirror always on.

Fifth displacement: jungle, its tangle, its greens insurmountable. The region has many names: The City of Snakes, The Fortified Houses, Stone Houses, and the Palisade, where they slipped the mirrors between leaves and vines, reflecting the undersides of vines and leaves, ricocheting a living verdigris that intensified the humidity of the seething greenery.

At Palenque the lush jungle begins. It's the reinvention of color torn into morning tearing in turn through the history of the word *color*, which, Smithson claims, means to cover, to hide, to conceal, as well as to save something in a small box called a mirror.

There's another version of the origin of the place name Yucatán: *Mac'ubah than* (we do not understand)   why it is 1517 and why these Spaniards are turning into the veins of these leaves and vines that keep on turning. A mirror displaces everything for eons. These days, mirrors occur whenever a plate of float glass is silvered, then backed by a layer of copper and then by one of paint, sealing in the light.

The jungle begins at Palenque, pours into the mirrors, and then overflows into windows, which are mirrors that no longer look back.

Sixth displacement: Agua Azul: a series of gentle cascades, the highest only 20 feet in the Xanil River running swiftly in its tangible turquoise and its blue measure of cloud, the cirrocumulus tracing in its feathers, the striations of wind layered among the tarnished surfaces of air folded into sand, like a small congregation reading light and replying in kind, the twelve aligned   and then the sun gets in your eyes. They arrived

in a single-engine plane, subject—as is everything but a mirror— to gravity. He mentions it particularly—molten river, iron water, stone lake while the plane's broken window acted as a third wing.

Seventh displacement: Yaxchilán: because they're tucked among the branches of a tree, a strangely haunting sheath among a site of ancient monuments—for instance, a large stone stele that archeologists from who knows where took out of the place in dugout canoes, but then, not able to get it on a plane, brought back again. The Yaxchilán displacement is by far the greenest and the only one vertical among its shadows in ruin. The architectural wreck of roots and vines gripped and finely patched

in watercolor   diffused throughout water   is a mirror
that the sun has entered   row by row   blinding now   one by one

the row of mirrors   rebuilds the interior.   By this point in the project, the displacements have become a kind of charged cartography, mapping light as a shattering of the cardinal points that can nonetheless be traced through its calligraphic itinerary, the mirrors tracking a legible geometry.

Eighth displacement: Arrived at the Usumacinta River, wondering what on earth the Island of Blue Waters could be. And before us, a river running through a curve, keeping the sweep in motion in each reflection in the mirrors placed errantly down a slope in wandering. Within any mirror, there's always another that looks out over a different world.

What shored up the river shored up the mirrors that shored up time. To shore as a verb, as another way to land, so that everything that fell onto any one of them fell also into our eyes. How delicately we now read in the sun, staring full west, the twelve of us, stuffing the sun back into itself.

Ninth displacement: near Sabancuy, into the right and left of it; never will they match, and the mirror is here to prove it. Here, we're back in the green of it, mangrove of the gravenly, the issue of inches of growth per hour, and the mirrors full of the same hours, but headed off elsewhere. We see, down in their deeps, that different sky and its different time, and a sun that never stops falling thought   through an open earth.

George Shiras
The Heart is the Dark

1871, summer, two days' walk with a Native American guide to
Whitefish Lake, about 20 miles southeast of Marquette, Michigan,
fairly within the realm of romance every summer for the next 70
years, there is a deer caught in the bright light of ignited magnesium,
there is a deer grazing at the water's edge, its reflection ruffling up
its coat, there are two white deer searing the darkness, there is a
lynx on the shore of Loon Lake staring straight at us.

Shiras photographed the night. He was trying to photograph the
nocturnal life of forest animals, which he did as well, but above
all, he photographed night as a material substance, and aslant;
it's in his backgrounds that night is caught in all its drift and grip,
in all its utter lack that shrieks, layered over sky. July 23, 1898:
deer, tail-white in lake of same, some taut line from eye to brain,

the eye holds tight, anchoring the line to the far shore in a mind
that night made precisely funambulist, precarious, all these animals
in their private skies climbed on through, a constellation of glinting
mammals merely startled for a moment on their ancient ways.

Shiras had hunted since childhood and only began taking photographs so that he could continue hunting beyond the end of hunting season without breaking the law—something perhaps personally pertinent, as he was, himself, a lawyer. And had a sense of law as, above all, a deep and steady pulse driving a core held in common among all creatures in all their numbers, be they heron, raccoon, or deer upon deer upon deer. Small owl with its eye on something even smaller.

Caught infinitely in the immediacy of their living. Which turned Shiras away from hunting and toward looking, resulting in a definitive conversion from gun to camera, acutely aware of their contradiction: The one ends the animal's life instantly; the other extends it indefinitely.

Which is not to say eternally—the animal remains tied to time, but in a way that lets time itself thin a bit. Jean-Christophe Bailly, in his introduction to the catalogue for the 2015-16 exhibition of Shiras's nocturnal wildlife photography at the Musée de la chasse et de la nature in Paris, says directly: "They are not 'timeless," but he places them in an "animal time" that he finds quite different from our own.

Perhaps it's that these photographs splice the two modes of time, the human and that of another animal, and they do so, ironically, by stopping them, as if stopping the two modes at the precise instance of their intersection fuses them, allowing those living in one to join, however briefly, the other. Perhaps it's the suddenness, embodied in the dramatic contrast of lighting, as if light was, in fact, nothing but the shock of stopped time.

Shiras wasn't the only one extending the hunting season via photography; there was, in the late 19th century, an emerging sub-genre that considered these photos as hunting trophies, and magazines such as *Forest and Stream* were publishing them. Shiras's unique contribution to the genre was the night. There's a raccoon out on a limb over Whitefish Lake, date unknown. There are two muskrats crossing a body of water on a slender twig, Yellowstone Valley, Montana. The body resounding, a bell within a blackness startling presence into the precision of attention.

And perhaps such photography, such a shock of sight, constitutes the apogee of attention—attention as the occupation of the other, an attendance on her or his presence so entire that it becomes your own.

So he stopped hunting and devoted more and more time to writing articles encouraging other hunters to abandon their guns in favor of the camera. Again, perhaps the addition of framing, the restriction of the field that's inevitable in a photograph, emphasizes the animal's own agency, focusing it in a way that manifests its centrality, which might, in turn, have allowed Shiras to see animals in a radically different relationship to their surroundings—now the center of the scene, subjects directing their own gaze, rather than the object of his.

And their surroundings included him, not as an outsider, but as an integral part of the whole, emanating a care rooted in night's language of gestures, glances, reflections, refractions. The syntax of darkness articulates each motion through the sound it makes through the air it displaces—the wing of a moth shifting a bird in its sleep. Or the owl, nocturnal, mute, which is its greatest resource, and its acute ear, its surest weapon and isolation—*Snowy owl perched above Whitefish River*, 1900, how the dark will echo, and the response be always a texture.

He spent most of his nights outside. He spent the light of his eyes in giving his eyes into the eyes that met his across a lake. The site of seeing established, composing countryside as the flank of an as-yet-inconceivable animal striding lightly through the soft, dark breath, the shadow in the heart of the shadow of his hand, the breathing hand that is, in fact, a camera taking optical measure in various dimensions that branch out from and endlessly complicate those hands.

Shiras traveled widely; he stopped practicing law in 1905—*that I might be free to interpret the laws of nature rather than those of man*—and devoted himself increasingly to his photography. Gliding over the black water in the quiet of a canoe, against the background of wings rowing through the air overhead, the footsteps of a raccoon, deft, across a log, skating over the sky and its blinded stars, a camera mounted in the bow.

He was an early experimenter in flash photography and the first to use a trip-wire trigger, showing animals wearing night like sheaths, moose half-dressed in light, Loon River, 1903, a beaver hauling her leafy branch into a dam, date unknown. And behind her, night goes on forever in a way that daylight never can.

Shiras used a modified version of a hunting technique employed by the Ojibways called jacklighting—a bright light is placed in the bow of a boat; the animal looks up, fixed by the light, the light firing the eyes that shoot it back again. The Ojibways used fire in a pan; Shiras used a kerosene flare.

Once the animal's attention is caught, you spray magnesium over three spirit lamps, which burst into flame, blinding the animals, including the people, and the boat glides on.

Jacklighting for hunting was eventually outlawed throughout most of North America because it was considered "unsportsman-like."

From the early 1890s on, Shiras became a more and more dedicated conservationist and used his years in the Pennsylvania legislature (1889 to 1890) and as a congressperson in the U.S. House of Representatives (1903-1904), to forward the cause. In later years, he featured prominently in several preservation projects—the Petrified Forest National Monument, 1906; Mount Olympus National Monument, 1909, the 1918 Migratory Bird Act, and the 1925 Shiras Gun Law, discouraging poaching by making it illegal to carry a gun in hunting areas outside of hunting season.

There is also a Shiras moose—*Alces alces shirasi*—a species that he discovered in Canada. *Moose grazing on roots of aquatic plants*, Matagamasi Lake, Ontario, 1904, peacefully huge with dead trees behind, and behind them, more and more night; it piles up without weighing down, but instead lifts off from the rolling shoulders and the trees.

A second later, all would be terror, the blinding light, the blinded moose, the striking noise, the animal leaping in all directions at once. Shiras noted that often the animals would not return to the spot or take the same path again for weeks or even months.

Doe across water   now   take your feather   and lift
the boat   into brilliance   now row
through your own ether   fawn after   it's over

and the legend of strange suns   that live only an instant
the legend of a boat that is itself immeasurable   distance
it must take the animal   whole minutes   maybe dozens
to get back their night vision during which they're incredibly vulnerable

Three white-tailed deer leaping to escape, Michigan, c. 1920, balletic desperation, the panic of complete articulation and a choreography of light against night that gives everything eyes.

Albino porcupine on a floating log, Whitefish Lake, 1905, a study of whites all studying themselves. And albino deer: *Albino stag in the forest*, Grand Island, Michigan, date unknown, his own beacon, so much lighter than the lit leaves above him. *Three deer and an albino deer*, Grand Island, Michigan, likely the same one leading three does, seeming to glow from within.

Cutting a bright slice across the lake, animal in length, a caution of lanterns, of antlers, among an orchard of wild oak. *Moose in the morning*, Nictau Lake, New Brunswick, 1907, gliding straight toward us, the mist luminous across the water behind him, perhaps all the light he needed.

The English translation of the title of Jean-Christophe Bailly's essay for the exhibition catalogue is *In the Heart of the Dark Night*; the original French title is *L'Intérieur de la nuit*; the choice of the word *heart* as a metaphor for *center*, rather than using the more literal *interior*, makes darkness into a body, but as darkness is both edgeless and endless, every point within it must, therefore, be its center, which means that night is an entity composed of nothing but its own heart. And what is a heart? You could say that it's what both drives a system and keeps time for that system. Or that, more simply, it's the rhythm that gives rise to life, or even more simply, a recognition that it is rhythm itself that gives rise to life and is the will that becomes the muscle to ensure it. Why it is night and not light that does this, I don't know, but I assume that it's because light constitutes another, as yet undiscovered, organ.

André des Gachons
The Sky in Time

The sky in a time of trees and fields with a fine layer of watercolor making it waver, as if seen in the distance, as if walking away, in the way that walking is always a way into a sky in a time of landscape made in and of the sky.

To paint in watercolor is to paint in weather. On a blue day, say, January 18, 1916, the wind headed north-northeast, and the blue hills separated from the blue sky by a strip of pink, and in the foreground, green openly rolling softly toward trees. The sky in a time of war is no less peaceful over fields.

André des Gachons painted thousands of watercolors of the sky over La Chaussée-sur-Marne during the First World War—and long after—in the peace of plain air. You whistle it, and it becomes an *aire*, and a small shard of calm passes through the softer tissues. Or you sing it out loud. Or you call out to a friend at the top of your lungs, as you sit with your brush, holding on. These are all uses of sky. He is sitting in a field with his back against a tree noting the minute details that make this day distinct from every other, layer after layer, of color in water, which is the essential feature of the sky; as it gathers, it wanders in a faintly scored aeration as three crows uncross it.

It's almost evening, and des Gachons is now sitting in the Tuileries watching the lampposts that light the paths, one by one, come on. It is 1921, and the war is gone. A single bat flickers its crisp silhouette, that odd effect of dusk in which the sky is paler than it's been all day, and yet there is so much less light in it. In its dusty evening, in its October, later and later, in its rare shelter, in which children are playing in the dark.

Born in 1871, André des Gachons was painting landscapes by the age of six, and by the age of 18 was living in Paris, studying at the Académie Julian. He seems to have had a romantic, maybe even dramatic, character and made a solid place for himself in the Symbolist movement. He studied with both Bouguereau and Puvis de Chavannes, and his work had gained enough of a reputation by 1895 that an entire issue of the review *La Plume* was dedicated to him, and, in the same year, he had a solo show in the *Salon des Cent*.

In keeping with the Symbolist ethos, his early work is simply dripping with meaning. How interesting, then, that he chose, and fairly abruptly, to shift completely to a practice based on extreme literality, painting scene after scene that means nothing but itself. Which is the essence of the weather—it simply is, and, in fact, is the very assertion of *isness*, the manifestation of a moment, that which makes time tangible, increasing its immanence until it's ubiquitous. After 1905, des Gachons painted nothing but the sky. By 1903, he had drifted away from the Parisian art world and had begun a rather hermetic life with his family on a farm near the banks of the Marne. In 1913, he established his first meteorological observation station and that year joined a national network of over 2,000 volunteer weather observers who sent detailed data daily to the *Bureau central météorologique*.

Aside: the pale, pale wheat of sky, and I wait. Often at a crossroads as the light is falling away, I wait, never crossing, and watching, the crossing, the away.

A measure, once familiar, can be both intimate and tender. He arranged his instruments according to size in an evenly spaced line, not only a thermometer and a barometer, but also an anemometer to detail the wind, a pluviometer to measure the rain, and a hygrometer, which used a single strand of hair to gauge the likelihood of same.

Des Gachons' brother Louis was a printer, and with him, he designed a form, 20 x 30 cm, with charts for recording the temperature, the atmospheric pressure, the velocity and direction of the wind, and the density (if any) of the clouds.

Two frames, about 10 x 15 cm each, were left at the bottom of the form so that he could translate that series of numbers into two watercolor landscape sketches, looking in each of two directions, thus extending the territory of meteorology by insisting on the sensio-aesthetic as a determinate dimension. At that time, of course, he could have simply taken a photograph, albeit not in color until much later. But working in watercolor underscores the corporeal, insisting on weather as something experienced by the body alone and never the mind. We take it in hand and from there, occupy its entirety, rising up into it, in which, in an infinitesimal layer, we are enveloped; we become its touch; there is no difference between the weather and us.

When the German army introduced the use of gas as an offensive weapon on April 22, 1915, the budding science of meteorology suddenly became extremely pertinent. This sudden need to predict the wind, unwittingly and lethally transformed, shows weather once more directing all human behavior without ever appearing to appear therein.

June 23, 1915, wind headed NE, a warm 20 degrees, and to the west, a clearing sky reveals patches of pale white and paler yellows above a farmhouse that probably has nothing to do with it—a tile roof that, nonetheless, oddly matches two patches of late light in deep peach off to the left. Whereas the trees, they are an integral part—they stand behind and loom beyond, the trees that extend the farm and yet also hold it in, one tree in particular, on the far right, rising to a spire.

While a moment later, in a sketch to the north, the clouds, a phalanx, enter, fragile, stuttering through a phantomatic launch and flaunting lightly whiter streaks, vertiginous, which means rain in the paint that sees through air.

January 9, 1916 was one of only three days on which des Gachons noted the effects of the war on the sky. He was 35 kilometers away from the German advance into Champagne and wrote in the margins of the form for the day: "The sky during and after the attack was perfectly normal and evenly homogeneous." And later: "Have the clouds coming from the front been affected by the bombs? I don't think so."

And February 17, 1916: wind from the north; temperature at 5 degrees with a sunset, coral into lime, climbing to a deep pink and then lavender for the rest of the sky of skeletal trees in the foregrounded green.

And yet if you turn to the west, the gradations of green from the center line forward are balanced by graduated yellows up into their purple; it's the trees, or rather their lines of force, that hold it all together, and, as the horizon is a perforation, he had the brazen inclination to let one thing see through another—through these trees thus the hills; through the hills, the river cuts.

Another of his instruments was a kite that he sent up to the trace the currents in the sky. And drift into sight- or torrent—sometimes the wind tearing in rages the kite to pieces scattered across a riverbank on hold.

And by five o'clock, if you turn toward: February 18, 1916: Wind and thunder from the north, and looking west at 5:05, a band of yellow (visible breeze) in the sky between two skies of grey.

Sky volatile, sky made of nothing but light, even wind, which we picture white, a sky in shreds. Or shredded sight wherever and when atmospheric pressure is split into seconds that were whole at the time the clouds thinned out, skidded into and across a white staccato sliced and increasingly silent; they silence the eye.

On the basis of literally years of observation, des Gachons established a catalogue of clouds, finding ten distinct kinds:

Cirrus: among the more ethereal frothed crystal

Cirrocumulus: in higher states of spun grain

Cirrostratus: masking the refracted sun in a hall of mirrors

Altocumulus: appearing as sugared almonds when the rain has melted

Altostratus: often the entire day

Nimbostratus: shredded at the heart of the breast of it

Cumulonimbus: a clearing, a lantern, a circus—just the words, with the things held at bay

Stratocumulus: by the armful, drawn by a child staring out a window

Cumulus: the tower that results in blue moves off

Stratus: washing across the solar plate, grinding down the edge of the sea

Seen 3 May 1916, rising wind from the southwest, a temperature of 18 degrees, hygrometry 70; to the west-northwest, pyramidal blue, growing against a green underscored and left ascendant—one could even say "clouds rampant." Every cloud, our oliphant.

Zineb Sedira
Lighthouse in a Sea of Time

3 part video installation

Part 1

The piece opens at night with an oddly bright amber bird flying by against a background of dark hills.

This first part of the work consists of four screens on which moving images of short duration are intermittently projected. The bird appears on the screen in the lower right.

The four screens often show echoes, often enlarged details, of other screens, just slightly off-set in time and scale.

Another bird passes, and then is enlarged on the screen to the left, at which point we see that, in fact, it's actually a patch of light rippling across the facing cliff at regular intervals.

Images flow and juxtapose across the screens; sometimes all are occupied at once, sometimes only one or two or three.

And then it's dawn, very calm, with clouds building up out to sea. A chain-link fence runs down to the shore, with a bird perched on almost every pole.

Cap Caxine Lighthouse, built in 1868 along the coast just outside Algiers, a long cobblestone path lined with deep green trees leads up to the lighthouse and the long white building below it.

Two men walk out into fog and head off, blending in, becoming less and less distinct and more and more the weather itself.

Rough waves crashing on a rocky shore with a line of tiny lighted windows stretched out along the low cliffs in the distance.

Cubic magnifying lens, an incisively sliced and blinding beam, cutting in, and into the lens itself, built of concentric glass circles, which in turn, circle the surrounding country.

Shots showing something of the structure of the lens, incredibly complex, suggesting the eye of an insect, so faceted and refractively active.

Then the images shift to the Cap Sigli Lighthouse, built in 1906, along a relatively uninhabited stretch of coastline some 100 or so miles away. Its light shines 25 miles out to sea.

From that high up, you can see far down the coast and the endless waves, the rhythm of days.

Another dawn. Someone flicks a curtain open across a brilliant window, all wrist.

Another window, this one spotted with rain, is echoed on the next screen by rain now running down in streams, while on the next, the camera backs up to give us a longer shot of the storm blowing through trees.

And the huge lens turning, reflected on yet another window and thus also in the reflected sky.

Followed by the pale shadow of parallel bars gliding calmly across a pale wall because another window that we can't see is opening.

An image of an arched glass door pouring warm buttered light out across a stone porch.

Evening seen through the rotating panes of the lamp, its shadow cast and seeking a place to land.

And then the scale shrinks, and we're looking at a pair of binoculars with french windows reflected in one of the lenses.

A hand holding a blue pen fills a sheet of paper with precise, tight writing, keeping a record of everything that goes on at the light.

Books on a bookshelf, on the cover of the first one: *Registre de Phare* (pronounced *far*).

The books contain pages and pages, going back decades, making a note of the rotation of keepers and the times when the light is turned on and off—often in winter, it's not before 8 am.

The lighthouse seen from land, through a lacework of barren branches.

A white boat passes far offshore; in fact, it's the only time we see a vessel out at sea, which seems ironic as, of course, boats and ships are the only reasons that a lighthouse exists.

There are 27 lighthouses along Algeria's 750-mile coastline, all with their keepers, working in a rhythm of relay and collaboration to carry out a wide range of functions all focused on the night, for that, of course, is when a lighthouse comes alive.

Part 2: *The Life of a Lighthouse Keeper*

It's a job that, in much of the world, is now handled remotely and automatically, so in this project, Zineb Sedira is also documenting a disappearing way of life.

In which we see that many of the fragmentary sequences that make up part 1 are either extracts or outtakes from this filmed interview with Karim Ourtemach, known as Krimo, now in his early 50s, who has been a lighthouse keeper at Cap Sigli since 2005.

His story is striking—having, when times were tough, taken to camping in a small stone hut below the Cap Sigli lighthouse, he began wondering about the life of the lighthouse keepers, and, after much observation, decided that it was a dream, and so it became his dream, and though the details of the story are not given in the film, he did, in fact, become one of the keepers of the Cap Sigli Lighthouse. We are in the presence of a man who is—I want to say *happy*, but that's too frivolous a term—this is a man who has arrived. At what he calls paradise. He's a painter, and often spends the entire morning drawing, then paints at night. And a fisherman when the sea is calm. His boat is blue, the same blue as the sky, and as the shutters and doors of the building where they live. *I will never move out of the Cap Sigli Lighthouse.* He speaks of the peace and of the wild landscape that he feels is a part of him. I will never leave here because I am here in the sense that it is what rather than where I am.

Krimo washing the huge windows of the lantern room, his sweeping gestures over the glass, a kind of choreographed semaphore, which is indeed a signaling, but this time inward, in toward the great lamp. The cleaner the windows, the farther the light.

Krimo then walking through the courtyard at the bottom of the lighthouse, where the lighthouse keepers live, where they go back into the kitchen and cook something for dinner—and over dinner, they talk—about what's gone wrong—with the optics, the mechanics, what's gone wrong with the light—often a matter of weather, and what storms have brought down what lines and what myriad other systems would, in turn, be brought down by that.

He says that they *sleep with one eye open*; in fact, all the keepers sleep facing a window that looks directly out on the light because a break in its rhythmic sweep will wake them up.

It's often in winter, when there are power cuts and shortages—insufficient electricity can cause the lamp to stop turning, and then they have to climb to the top and turn it by hand for the rest of the night.

They have visitors from time to time—he often asks them to stay for lunch or dinner. They sign a register with their name, the date, and any comments they wish to make—*Très heureux d'avoir visité ce phare*—*Many thanks for your hospitality and the chance to see your beautiful coastline*—and from the poet Tahar Djaout, *I didn't know that between Azeffoun and Béjaïa there was such a miraculous place, which teaches us that a faraway spot can also be the center of the world*.

A lighthouse, no matter how anchored its foundation, is always teetering between the literal and the figurative—lighthouse as savior: how many ships have not broken up on these rocks?

Lighthouse as witness: history in all its bitterness, pierced by an exigent spear.

Lighthouse watching over us and the fine line between sea and land. Lighthouse as shepherd, keeping separate things separate.

To spend your whole life tending a light.

Part 3: *La Montée*

A spiral staircase—the video begins with long, upward views of the entire extent, the ascent, photographed so that it's just slightly off-set. The mar in that perfection keeps the whole thing in motion so that the stairs never end.

It opens with Zineb Sedira walking up to the Cap Sigli Lighthouse; we see her arriving through her reflection in a glass cabinet that faces the door. She starts climbing, counting each step, stopping from time to time for breath. The camera follows her from the top. Elsewhere there are stills of the same staircase taken from the bottom looking up at the ceiling of the tower and at the light shining down from its center.

Irving Petlin
A Night in the Sun

His June 2018 show titled *Un soleil dans la nuit* at Galerie Jacques Leegenboek, Paris, curated by Nadine Fattouh—thirteen pastels on paper—was thematically based on four of Simone Weil's recurrent themes: *Attention, Work, Force*, and *The Beauty of the World*.

The *Beauty of the World* series at first seems to be entirely fire, but then burns more and more into sky. Yet by morning, what calm, a gold caught in the trees streaming through it, the smallest speck exploded into the mist now warm and warming the trees migrating through veils of it, through shores turning to shelter and the sheltering water and the waterfall turning to sound. You can watch it turning, slowly into it, in the early sun.

Weil: *The forms of love implicit in God*

Work, where the recurrent image is a flight of stairs; may it follow you home, and the stair turning too in the palm of your hand, this work of the end is also made of hands from a certain distance there's real light in the lamp at the top of the pole at the top of the steps where the soul waits alone.

Attention—to the other, which opens a small pale box over the left shoulder—*Work*—to which we submit, glitch, and slip out of ourselves—*Force*—which must be refused and refused its war while the *Beauty of the World* turns always toward.

Attention to the rhythm of the steps in their labor through the gold that living into grey turns to green, rhythm of the cracking sky, its cracks not equidistant yet creating a pattern that turns to something walking in long bolts that amount to extremely fine openings, regular as time. An horizon along which a silhouette exits to the left.

Work: Smoke, now a boat. Everything vertical all over the sky is somehow now the sum total of the boat, with all it carried, now empty, on the empty shore, an oar on its own all over the lake.   It used to be a sea. And thus are things. Shocked by scale.

Far Study said later in the heat of the day. *Far Study* hand-written along the bottom of the sheet of paper in a script that suggests, not urgency, but certainty.

The papers all come either from India or Nepal; he found them at New York Central Art Supply. The laid-lines in the Indian papers are curiously wavy, and here and there, long curling fibers look at first glance like pencil lines, like someone idly thinking into the structure of the paper.

He got the last sheets available in the U.S. Handmade paper is always a collaborator, he says; because of its irregularities, it actively participates in the work. And pastel, complementarily, accepts improvisation, a play of give and resist that results in sharps, almost sparks, or sudden runs, often running after something streaming through the dark.

Work: They walk amid the white horse with its own ghost; they walk in a line up the stairs and the dogs don't end. What is your interest in Simone Weil? Where did you find the boat? There is no one in it, and the dogs go off at a run.

In the next one the horse is still alive and its ghost stands off to the side as the people in a line walk up the stairs on the left to the left of the sea.

Irving Petlin gets his pastels from La Maison du Pastel in Paris; they make all their pastels by hand following techniques developed by Henri Roché, who took over La Maison Macle, which had dealt in art supplies, including pastels, since 1720. In 1865, when Roché bought the business, their clients included Whistler, Degas, and Chéret. Roché was a pharmacist who had studied under Pasteur (who, in fact, was also a pastel artist), but Roché's real love was the visual arts, and he became more and more interested in applying his knowledge of chemistry to making the perfect pastel. He worked closely with Monsieur Macle, learning his techniques, and by 1878, he was the sole person in charge. Changing the name to La Maison du Pastel, he decided to stop selling anything else.

Weil: *it is beautiful, and so it must be true*. Trees drifting through a shore of morning and the waterfall (still) turning to sound that you watch slowly turning to sun on the back of your hand.

Roché took over from Macle with 100 colors—though *color* is not the right term; La Maison du Pastel uses the term *nuances* when discussing them, which is no doubt better, as a given color is always made in a range of nine shades going from dark to light. By 1887, Roché had 500 *nuances*; his son joined him in 1906, and by the outbreak of WW1, they had 1000. Roché *père* died in 1925, mixing up pastels until practically his final day, when Roché *fils* took over. After his death in 1948, his widow and three daughters kept up the production, always further developing their product and always through direct consultation with a great number of artists, querying their needs and fine-tuning their wares to address them.

By the late 1990s, the three sisters were all over 80 and were looking about for a likely successor, which they found in a much younger cousin, Isabelle Roché, in her early thirties at the time and working as a chemist in industrial petroleum. Today, she runs the business with her partner, Margaret Zayer, at 20 rue Rambuteau, where the concern has been located since 1912, though they make the pastels themselves in their workshop out in the country. As of summer, 2018, they're handling 1320 shades.

Pastel has the oddest transparency—it's ostensibly opaque, but across uneven paper, it veils down through the layer below to the layer below that, a sequence of brittle glazes that offers a different way to juxtapose pure colors—as if exploring the divisionists' suggestion that the eye can blend colors to a vibrancy that the hand cannot, but with a depth that includes a vertiginous drift.

Pastel, says Petlin, has a very particular relationship to time— within it, there's no going back, and it's much quicker; it moves across the paper with a granular fluidity, melting with integrity in the physical sense of the word.

Cadmium green was the first new color that Isabelle Roché made; Petlin came in one day with a tube of oil paint, hoping to find exactly the same shade in a pastel. To translate a color from one medium to another is to make a new color, a color suddenly alone, which in its isolation, shifts it off the map, allowing us to be lost—how much farther one can wander as long as the shade doesn't yet have a name.

They made him the cadmium green. And then, one evening over dinner, presented him with a gift of several shades of gold.

Thinking, they said, that there is something Byzantine in his skies. And in Weil's as well, though something broke in hers to crack the gold into a concept of God, it all going warm, the sky she lived under in Spain, the sky that she polished with a soft blue cloth until it ached.

Metallic pastels are much harder to make. They are 80-90% pigment (mica-based treated with oxides), so there's very little else holding them together—they want to pollinate, infiltrate, integrate—they seem to come off the paper toward you, a floating layer veiling the yellow in the lamp, now a single man, alone on the stairs.

The tents of a nomadic camp are scattered against the horizon, and what is that metallic green? And are they carrying something up the stairs that we can't see?

Weil: *The good is the motion by which we break away from ourselves as individuals*, which is the stair in words carried all that way, linking the stairs to the plain. Simone, known for the awkwardness of her hands, also climbing the stairs in her painfully studied script.

Migration, and the loss inherent therein, has been one of Petlin's persistent themes for over thirty years. (Simone sailing to America with her parents in 1942.) In a boat, in a line, in a long distance that starts at the throat where a blue crashes into the otherwise greens and apricots and a searing white.

Weil in a nutshell: Love is a face that makes the world beautiful by turning continually toward it.

Where the gold slips slightly out of sight of the hand

as we watch the stairs ascend, and with them, a man.

Fugitive, they say, of a color that can't stand up to the sun.

Back at the show three days later I notice that all five of the pieces from the *Beauty of the World* series have sold (which, in fact, the gallerist told me, all sold on the first night), but neither of the two from the *Force* series. And one from *Work* and one from *Attention*.

Pastel has a broader scope, a more acute impact, Petlin says; a painting has to be huge to feel huge, but pastel covers more space, can twist scale; a relatively small piece can cover a whole wall.

Work: Chicago: His father got up every morning at 5 am to go to his shift in a factory; he'd get up then too in order to have a few hours to draw before the hectic schedule of the day began and watched his father walk out the door.

On some of those cold mornings, he drew nothing but trees. And, now in his eighties, Petlin has developed a signature tree; it unravels into the sky becoming an inverted structure all tangled in sun. At the moment, this tree is standing on the bank of a river pulling down until the sky rests on the water, which moves off to the left, taking the reflected leaves along with it.

Along walks it. As they lead the white horse on—its translation toward—years in the making, a lake also and calmly, the shiver on its surface also traveling with the horse now approaching the shore on her own and her living.

So walk the new horse down. Say it into stone. If the stair is stone, it doesn't end, if the child in its arms ends in mid-air

Only beauty can save the world.

The beauty of the world is a tangible thing resting in the palm, for instance, appearing for a moment as a fever of river that at first glance you think is a flame; the beauty of the world pours across the bank, the horse now amid stars is also the one broken up in the shafts of sun through the trees along the shore, themselves made entirely of light with the beauty of the world in the background because it stretches out beyond, extending your range of sight, actually increasing its size, it unties.

To now inhabit these trees. Now they are three in dozens of greens. To live in peach in between, with a line at the bottom handwritten: *Esperons des trois arbres*, writing their own hands.

The beauty of the world also includes a paler form, a child, transparent, a clarity bending slightly forward, the bright streaks coming in reflected into skin.

And it includes a bright red bird, a red circle, and a horse that now takes up half the sky. Color wanders, lost among them. Others are remembered, there on the stairs.

Renee Gladman
Acsemic Cities

A city in the distance is always something toward which

a city in the distance is always rising up against

and rising within is always a city whose name is always on the tip

recalibrating the angle of the hand poised over the paper.

The hand puts down the pen and goes off to make a cup of tea

while the distance of the city increases

the distance between the hand and its own cemantic possibilities.

Renee Gladman's drawings could be anything, but they happen
to be cities.

They are vertical cities, built of sheer ascension, ascending across
great expanses. And still expanding, hand over hand, the intricate

fingership, gestured an acrobat, and executed with a newly sharpened needle. Most often in pencil, .5mm or .38—*I like the kind where you can take off the end and sharpen the point* to a diamond tip, which can cut through pretty much anything, including a diamond

        embedded in the graphite, the finest scintillations of all the lighted windows receding across the plain. It was a city moving away, called by others to which it was linked through an intricate network of threaded silence emanating from late streetlights and the darkness honing in, getting closer and closer to the shadow of a walker, who, beneath a wash of ink, occupied it all, so that the shadow could think.

Gladman refers to buildings as *other kinds of beings* also thinking (*thinking takes the shape of buildings*) that only architecture creates the possibility of coming in.

The entire west wall of Gladman's studio is a bank of greenhouse windows, through which sunlight washes in and across the paper across which precise characters migrate themselves into habitable structures.

We came into the first city after a long walk across a bright plain fired with sand and sun, and so, to come upon an entire city built of rungs of carbon spun with hematite—the delicate stairs, almost all of them spiral, the bridges, fragile and aerial, spanning from tower to tower, at times disappearing into solid marble cliffs and from there through room after room lit only by sunlight suffusing walls, paper-thin.

As Gladman says, *Architecture again, it always comes back to that*. Entire countries in which there is nothing not arcing or texturing in a crystalline accrual; we wait for the salts to bind, and the tiniest bird, perfectly worded, breaks through the fine facade.

In her drawings, this break is an exploration of time (*Drawing was going into time*), a refusal to let it go straight, making it admit that it endlessly twists as it follows itself back through those long cool rooms of stone you can see through, and through them seeing an unlimited language that lives between words and emerges as graphic elaborations in which we, in turn, dwell in fluidity, for the city as written constantly shifts in dimension, a rift

along a fault line has determined many a landscape. As many a vertical fault has been traced by a finger down a plate-glass window looking out until the sky goes blank. Whereas there's never any sky in Gladman's drawings; the bank of west-facing windows looks out onto a forest that takes off from the top of a steep bank and extends to the top out of sight. In front of the windows, and flooded by a sheet of sun, is a desk lined with jars and glasses chock full of brushes, dozens and dozens, stained at their tips, if

color is always a choice of sky, and sky always a wash—a brush—of weather in the eye—so her cities float—city of signs, city of sentience, city faltering on pronunciation. A city that cannot quite be said and thus finds itself dependent on a hand and a line.

All drawing and all writing are necessarily made by hand and once inside, the hands multiply, splay, delta-like, feathering into living. Gestures of ash.

Within gestures of glass. A question of angle and curve, or a more general one of dispersal and its affinity for acute precision, a mist of crystal—with Gladman's hand precariously poised between the vegetal and mineral, constructing refracting cities throughout the spreading neuronal canopies of overflying trees.

And as if overhearing our very thoughts, a second city suddenly reigned above—we looked up into open, uncontrollable cathedrals, all sparkle and stark in their elemental assertion, infusing flint into the fevered greens that cleave and leave the leaves to dissipate into aerial meadows, intricate in their grasses interwoven, which, too, we suddenly find we are reading.

Which itself creates other hovering structures, which we meander, which is simply to pass the mind over a field that makes time wander

which is to say   you just let the hand go on   entirely on its own, which Gladman does, watching it from a distance, a mammalian instrument that can't help inventing alphabets, acsemic in their asymptotic approach to a semantic content whose constant retreat constantly increases the territory of signification. Tiny signs that braid the air in such a way that the signs made there

stay there—brittle phrases of metallic filaments—and the glancing blow of the sun off of any one of them—catch it right, and you've got a blind spot for days—as they, twisted or involuted or calligraphic, cartographic, or axiomatic, persist in their resistance to perspective—her drawings only rise.

We lived in the city as a matter of measuring. We lived in the city as a method of filtering. We filtered the finest grains of the slightest emanations we gathered from everything living, and distilled them.

In this way, it's the city that creates the *we* that we are—precipitated out of a landscape oversaturated with life—and only a city can orchestrate the throng of each body in relation to all others. And so we entered the second city with perhaps exaggerated expectations—and in light of that, we perhaps should not have been shocked by the light.   But why am I using

the past tense? Fear, I guess. But in fact, it glints audibly throughout the resounding hall where suddenly, here we are, which is just what all the tricks of popular theater, the traveling circus, you name it, are not

                              tricks at all. She draws the act of thinking, delineating an anatomical model of shelter, a plan drawn to scale that we can annotate into ourselves in perpetuity.

We still live in this city in which writing is drawing
                                        the living carefully
over every receptive surface.

We live in this city in which walking is mapping time with a diamond across glass, the sound of a skate across ice. We live in that slice with senses alight; in fact, the city climbs just like icebergs fracture, the deep slam of a calf breaking off; here, where they break only upward, and it's the sky that calves, and the hand that hears creates a haptic trace—touch as line become legible, not to the eyes, but to the body alone on an open plain that always precedes. *I like a pencil's relationship to the space behind it*

      which goes on back forever because a pencil is innately phantomatic, singing to itself through an inner phosphorescence.

Interviewer: *Do notions of ephemerality, fragility, or spontaneity even come into it at all?*

Gladman: *I wish I had more time*

We entered the third city as a ritual act of silent reading, which is to say that suddenly there were previously invisible structures still invisible, but now imbedded deeply within us. They climbed away inside of us, always upward—thin, gilded sequences with something silvered to their errance. We became it. It was and is our inhabitation—a precision only possible in pencil. Which alone can turn landscape into an acsemic panorama—miles and miles in all directions in the ultimate pleasure of writing without having to say a thing.

Gustav Klimt
Seventeen Summers

Summer enters a series of photographs, so often on a dock, perhaps 1903, Gustav Klimt wearing his painter's smock, a monk on a lark with friends, including two men in a boat, oars in their hands and the island of Litzlberg behind them.

You can tell that they're friends, which is what makes it summer, which becomes the texture of reception; a friend holds out a hand to a friend stepping off a boat, children in the background, distracted by something they're watching down in the water.

And now on the porch of a boathouse, 1904: Klimt and Emilie Flöge, the only land in sight, far off behind them, hills to the left.

In another photo, the large, soft nose of a horse takes up much of the upper right, and so the people beyond become calm, the lake laughing all over his face in the sun—

the softer boat—

—under arc—under willow or gliding up to the shore in the falling shadow, all pollen in shower. Lemon trees, too, or the lemon alone, inherently summer

in the palm of the hand. To simplify
a complex life. *Every morning just painting*, he wrote, "growing
trees."

Indeed, leaf by leaf and other friends, the *Sommerfrische*
spent with an extended network of three families united by
marriages and picnics, long walks, and wild hats around a table at
the edge of a lake.

Klimt and Flöge in a rowboat, photo undated,
Klimt, an oar left in his hand, and Emilie standing, the other oar
beside her, smiling, lined with shore—Flöge with her sweeping,
open overture, fiercely of summer, a sun of opinions, graciously,
but firmly, a boat in the anchor of her hands.

Emilie Flöge, an exceptionally independent woman and a leader
in the dress reform movement, which connected unrestrictive
clothing to the political emancipation of women, was the younger
sister of Klimt's brother's widow and was Klimt's constant
companion for the last 27 years of his life. Klimt collaborated with
her on numerous dress designs, such as the voluminous robes
they're both wearing, Flöge standing, facing us smiling, and Klimt
rowing in a photo with a crisp sailboat slicing brightly into the forest
in the background stretching to the horizon.

There's no indication that Klimt used any of these photographs
in his work, but they may have given him the occasion to rethink
proportion and put it at the service of the vast: *The Park* 1909—

the enormous fluidity of the tree—he understood how truly large
trees are—he spread it out with the flat of his hand, extended

the shadows into the shadowed, just as reflection dissembles or
sweeps the people,

> small and uncountable,

the people

> being swept up into the trees.

And Emilie—she stands, adjusting a sleeve—she too is under a
tree, and because the photograph is in black and white, her hair
blends into the leaves.

1898: with the Flöge family at St. Agatha, painting the weather,
the family central to the Austrian avant-garde, fin-de-siècle, where
it has just stopped raining in the orchard still under the sway of the
Vienna Secession, and as for the distance, he was already using
various optical devices to achieve a detail that ruptured scale and
unified the surface.

And Golling the year after, known for its gardens, terraces, and
waterfall—the paintings: *Morning by the Pond* and *Orchard in
the Evening* watching the hours cross the glass reflection of the
sun splitting open a tree.

That summer he adopted the format of the square and used it for
all of his landscapes from then on; in this way, he too dissolved the
distinction between portrait and landscape, thus asserting a place
as a living being, as breathing and moving, a body stretching in the
morning down a long avenue of over-arching elms, c. 1915. The
person at the very back of the photo, so small that the trees grow
taller as the figure disappears.

How many of his trees are larger than the sky. So many of his trees are why the frame was made

a broken thing

by giving way—by the trees arise—the tree as pure height. *Tall Poplars I*, 1900; *Young Birches*, 1900—it was a year in which we leaned back and looked up and found that there was a limit that the concept, but moreover, the fact

of a tree

let us slip past.

And suddenly, it's August again, so again, they pack up the clothes, the books, the paints, and the canvas—Klimt started his paintings on site, his days often beginning at 6 a.m., and often he would paint from a boat, a mist across the lake gliding sideways in a certain laterality that annihilates depth.

At the time, his landscapes were referred to as *atmospheric*; and the word *timeless* was frequently employed, which seems odd, as they are, in fact, about nothing but time and its fleeting resistance, about the length of a flicker that can get light to move water.

From 1900 to 1916, he spent every summer on the Attersee— at the Brewery Inn at Litzlberg until 1907, then at the Villa Oleander at Kammer until 1913, and then down on the south shore, where they stayed in the house of their friend Forester at Weißenbach.

Forty-six of Klimt's fifty or so known landscapes were painted at this lake—his compositions sighted from a long way off, and in fact, he made a viewfinder, which he called his "seeker," by cutting a square window out of a piece of cardboard, leaving a wide margin at the bottom by which he held it up to the distance,

moving it slowly up and down, left and right. He must have had one eye shut, which must have made him slightly squint, which must have made passersby wonder if he'd gotten something in his eye.

And later, looking across to the *schloss* (*Schloss Kammer on the Attersee I*, 1908), the light on the water is the light of the house— the bright white of its face, which must, just at this moment, be stricken by noon, which made someone turn around, and thus there's a face looking back over a shoulder asking

                  If

everything we're seeing is not actually paint or at least in part
     a handprint on the sun
alone
     summer is.

That said, very few of Klimt's landscapes that feature water include reflections. Exceptions: *The Litzlbergkeller on the Attersee*, 1912-16, and 1916, *Schönbrunn Park*. Perhaps it was simply that he rarely looked back. Perhaps, too, a view is always a driving force and one that's always headed forward, past the photographic evidence, suspended on its small peninsula: most of them painted through opera glasses or a telescope, the lens collapsing depth and making the view refuse to extend; instead

it climbs (there goes the sky) colonizing the sky, layered or erasing, leaf by leaf, so that in most of his works, there's no sky at all, or only a very thin strip way up at the top, so the light then must come from the painting itself, and so the world is lit by hand.

A slightly darker green beneath enters the weather, the drizzle all summer, all slight St. Agatha in the final years of meadows, up against a lake surrounded by centuries of light mist and a lighter almost celadon rising.

Some summers come with more weather than others: 1913: The broken green is a singing thing, a singing that we heard and turned, and there it was: Klimt in splinters slicing off light with a very small knife, slivers wherever a verdure is engendered and Klimt, face down in the green of it.

He was a man who never got used to the telephone, though he had one installed in his place in Vienna in 1912, but he wrote copiously— letters and postcards and more postcards—postcards that he also used to turn sketches into full paintings. And often he wrote, not on the back, but over and around the image, filling up the sky:

And when I pass through this room

making me yearn

amid rain.

And late in August, 1915 to Emilie: *It would have been very, very nice to be able to get away . . . I have half a mind to pack everything in and join you . . .* And a postcard to his sister-in-law 11 September, the same year: *After a summer of rain and wind, I am coming home tomorrow!*

Another postcard to Emilie, March 11, 1916: *The resplendent sun has arrived, making this almost a day of rejoicing! 'Crocus' or 'Krokus' are blooming in the garden, and the ground appears a starry sky*—One tends the eye as one tends the mind, choosing his studios according to the outside space they offered for planting flowers increasingly as he got older, the flowers in the background end in a slight rebuke at the bottom of a postcard: *No mention in your letter of the flowers in the region.*

His last summer at the Attersea was 1916. He scattered enormous trees all over in tiny pieces that landed in places that made them into places
and then walked out without thinking.

Later, Klimt at the oars and the boat with its own brittle idea of order, racing a leaf down a mirror.

He worked slowly, meticulously rising before anyone else into the empty house, into the summer that far north in which the question of morning is increasingly simply a tone on a pallet, a gravel path from which you could see the foothills of the Alps. A gravel path up which no one is walking. There are never any people in Klimt's landscapes, no animals, and so we must concede that it must be the landscape itself that is moving.

Tacita Dean
In Light of the Sea

"has receded into a further past than is strictly chronological"

will rain again	*and the pool of light*	*down will rain*
and will I face	*and will I*	*walk on back*

across the plain of water, drawn, minute, precise, a seascape in-finite, a glint of flight, a flint struck, run dumb allt or just the white voice of the white noise of the sea speaking across.
                                                                    The sea
is always across.
                      Does the boat make it or not?

A seascape, unlike a landscape though they both function by creating more distance than the scene could actually hold—makes you think you're outside the frame, but this is an illusion, and you think that's what soothes you, but it's not; it's the rocking of the clock in the sea.

Though best known for her films, Tacita Dean began her career making drawings; some early foundational ones were in chalk on two 4' x 8' blackboards, one above the other on her studio wall.

To draw is, into the ephemeral, a mark that began as a scar and then afar

becomes a verb.　　And just as a boat creates a shore
a ship, a rift in time, awakened by a jolt

the sea continued on.

And as such　　　in chalk lost　　　in the dark　　　erased

Often when I consider the desolation of the sea, I imagine it as a place unchanged by the passage of time, a rare prehistoric world where a human being can truly be lost.

was now a hand in fog

its name swept off

(was never heard)
holding up a lantern
as the chalk stormed on—

At one point, she did sixteen blackboards all about walking away. Walking erases—layer by layer—the past into a palimpsest, which is also a moving picture traveling through time also in layers adrift

and then retraced: *Sixteen Blackboards*, 1992 was one of her first major projects, and was in fact an early exploration of how to move an image through time—or rather how to get time to move an image onward—for it was through the progressional quality of these still images that she moved into film.

Dean made her first films with a Cannon Standard 8mm camera that had belonged to her father, himself the son of the founder of Ealing Studios. She was hoping to get lost.

And then she found a book: *Last of the Wind Ships*, in which an enterprising young woman with every intention of losing herself suddenly lost the sea.

And so further blackboards: *Girl Stowaway*, 1994, in which the young woman traveled from Port Lincoln to Falmouth in 1928 to sink off the coast at Starehole Bay. Who later wrote a memoir, *The Log of a Happy Girl*, of a chalk ghost of a woman somewhere

in the sea itself lost in thought became a ship constantly slipping along a gulf of light   that erased the face   that effaced the girl in a wreck of sun

In which are rooted Dean's twin interests in the analogue and the anachron. *But this fantasy belongs to the analogue world: the world where you could still get lost . . . Maybe getting lost, or rather disappearing out of sight, has become an anachronism ...*

I court anachronism.

The word, in one form or another, appears at least six times in *Selected Writings 1992-2011*, and the concept rules a number of her projects:

Kodak, 2006: *without a sigh or a nod to all we are losing*. In her film work, the materiality of the medium plays a central role, and she is wholly committed to film as opposed to other modes of getting images to move, such as video, though she realizes that film is, itself, a medium that's increasingly anachronistic, inexorably headed toward obsolescence—a word that appears at least ten times in the same volume. Some of her still projects, too: *GAETA*, 2015—fifty photos of Cy Twombly's studio printed on the last Cibachrome photographic paper available.

The hurtling toward history that haunts her principal medium seeps through to haunt her content as well: *I have this uncanny thing with filming things and then they disappear.* And seeps further into her daily life: *As soon as I like something, Shoof! It suddenly seems to disappear.*

Her 1991 film *Ztráta*, made in Prague, where the word means loss or disappearance: a young teacher writes it on the blackboard in capital letters, then wipes it off with a cloth and throws the cloth out the open window.

The analogue and the anachron—"to be at sea" is to be spatially lost in a homogeneously continuous world, just as the anachronistic is that which is lost in the homogeneity of time. With loss and limit inversely related, and both appearing as untouched by time as is time itself.

And though the sea may seem *unchanged by the passage of time*, that is not to be timeless in the transcendent sense of eternity, but is to *be* time, to be fused with all of time all at once through a presence that comprises all tenses.

For instance, *How to Put a Boat in a Bottle*, 1995: In trying to grasp the impact of the wreck of the ship on which the girl had stowed away, you make a tiny replica of the vessel, the *Herzogin Cecilie*, and then learn how to fold it, how to slip it through the neck of a bottle, and how to watch it unfold its alternate history, riding its sea of glass, raining in a sea of light, its own coast, which time will dust over, will lie in an infinitesimal layer of dust on water.

And is linked to *Prisoner Pair*, 2008, the pears grown inside the bottles of the fruit brandy known as Poire William. Makes the pear into a sea-going vessel. We see a single pear or a fleet of them making oceanic crossings that an ocean liner could not, nor the lightest ship

its sails dazed in light

as the light poured down

a calm

can be as dangerous as any storm.

On central California beaches up through the 1960s, brightly colored glass floats, made to hold up fishing nets off the Japanese coast, would occasionally wash ashore. And birds float across, and spiders and seeds on the wind, and all of them less vulnerable than the glorious, intricate, and infinitely sailing ships.

Disappearance at Sea, 1995, was first a blackboard series, which she then made into a film in 1996. In it, we are always looking outward, caught in a wash of the large, the lighthouse beside us, our guide. *I always choose situations where the light is very important. The light is always a character.* The light is always a house in which we arrange ourselves to live.

Go down

        said the ship

on down go

        No, said the ship

dressed in snow.

        Oh no

ship like this

        ever said yes.

David Hockney
The Four Seasons, Woldgate Woods,

four 9-screen video installations

There was a slow road
            and the road unfolded slowly, acutely, Hockney
had long been interested
              in inverted perspective

which places the vanishing point somewhere back there behind
you and going
            the road
down through trees
            the road only
slows the road on.
Nine cameras attached to the summer of 2010

and spring. He put it at the end. Here we pool the bloom. Here we
line the sight down the open eye down which the road only finely
goes, time into time

the tyranny of vanishing-point perspective
            . . . I've been obsessed with

the road that carried there a kind of splice, a prism that defines four forms of light, taut, walking on out, all viscous summer, tinsel winter ringing in the mind as down the road solely, the mind splits into nine.

So, slow down the road, no

green   if we take this as seeing has ever, for instance been in bright insistence, so immeasurably crisp

erupts in a leaf: Summer: Startling-smell-flower and trees flowering white trees flowering green, each changing each other in overlapping layers, these greens that build and filter, divide in flight, making color the entire substance of the season.

1 minute and 1 second into it, headlights pierce the surface, a needle threading fog, which light twists infinitesimally into the center screen through mist. It's the only time in all four seasons that another car passes. Hockney has said that it's isolated country, diffusing at its edges in the headlights fraying rain.

It's been raining, and it shines on the road. We're in a car we never see, and we never see the *we*, and yet this gaze is clearly communal, the multiplicity of perspectives, at its most literal, simply physical, suddenly makes the distilled landscape so quietly all one eye.

He mounted nine cameras on the front of a truck and drove incredibly slowly so that none of them match each tree as it passes   each leaf   a split-second   each branch

an integral part of the season and the density of foliage. The sequence sometimes begins with a line of trees migrating evenly off to the left, pacing their elsewhere, hypnotic as wind

in their slow-motion history of the ripe mist that's blooming from time to time he would leave early in the morning in blossoming hawthorn afraid of missing dawn.

By the time it's fall, it's all a halt of altered color starting to empty the empty sky coming down to touch, turns to sun on a road through a grove. It's been raining again which makes the light sink in

as it opens the road   deeper on russet   breaking on grey
the sun again making leaves into lanterns in the broadness of day
the tyranny of a single way   the tyranny of things too straight.

He once described entering the St. Gotthard tunnel as *living in one-point perspective hell*—He chose a road broken, dispersing its splinters. The resulting *Four Seasons* meticulously unstraightened with its holes in the foliage from left-over rain.

He made many of them, filming day after day, the nine cameras arranged on a grid, going on ahead, seeing more than could ever be seen by a single pair of eyes, each of the cameras set to a different exposure, and then recomposed on a computer.

Hockney spent countless hours on minute adjustments in a process he considered a version of drawing. To draw the edge of each into a scene that seems to hold us too in a center that grows.

And though throughout the series, we're constantly moving, we will clearly never arrive, but continue to shift in relation to the relative proportions of road and trees. *Chinese aesthetic theory had rejected the idea of a vanishing point by the eleventh century because it meant that you—the viewer—weren't there. You weren't moving. If you're not moving, in a way, you're dead.*

Four seasons ahead and four seasons receding before us—a theme that since antiquity has been used as an allegory for the migration of the soul, also tyrannized by a single vanishing point.

And so he broke each season into nine, with nine points each of vantage that vanish   in winter   snow falls off of branches which is recorded by the cameras as tiny blinding slices in the sky that fuse the blue   into the upper reaches   where the sun bends

the weight of flicker and shift   and quietly winter   makes us hear the silence inherent in sight.   37 seconds in, a large, black bird, raven or crow, floats upward from the bottom of the center screen lofts on across the road   and is absorbed by the snow of the upper branches   where the sun bends again   each season to its own conditions.   For instance, mist, he says, makes detail surge forth more sharply, and though this seems counter-intuitive, it may be that its enveloping conditions our acceptance

of three-dimensionality. Or makes us lean forward and focus with a heightened scrutiny. Or perhaps ensures a productive ambiguity that lets us participate, lets us incorporate something that sparks spontaneously through the electrical encounter between ourselves and the scene. And another bird in spring 3 minutes and 27 seconds in, also black—crow or raven—crosses

or it's the same one, heading in the other direction, swooning down from the upper left to nick the corner and then exit, just as we do, out the back of the screen into all the screens at once, all slightly off-set, they move un-rhymed, re-timed. In ancient Chinese aesthetic theory, it was, he said, called 'moving focus' embodied by the body as a lens calibrated to the speed of trees weaving sky, and the great trees hauling all of time along with them (*Trees don't follow the laws of perspective*) at the end of summer, veering very, very slowly off the road.

131

Frederick Law Olmsted
The Centrality of the Park

Olmsted saw parks as integral elements of the city, urban in nature (there is nothing that is not natural), and they certainly don't exist in the wild.

Park: land textured in art
Landscape: making what's close
look both far in the distance and well within reach.
By this we are increased.

Fredrick Law Olmsted, a farmer who chose his farm for the view, who became one of his country's first landscape architects almost by accident. He'd worked as an investigative reporter, publisher, abolitionist, mine supervisor, army hospital administrator, farmer, and writer, among other things, when the post came open for the superintendent of Central Park. Writing out the application by hand, he claimed:

"We see a million people of all backgrounds and stations, skating with a sun setting behind them through half a million trees." His initial plan was ten feet long and required tiny sketches in pencil of all the half million, so everyone who came by his house, from creditors to relatives to all of their children, was handed a pencil and set to drawing a forest marching off into another half million.

Olmsted and his partner, Calvert Vaux, were awarded the commission.

Central Park, March, 2019:   You stand on the edge looking in just at dusk   because I'm standing   looking at dusk coming into the park or emerging therefrom, dusk, a soft animal

without a body   that rises   to spread throughout the entire city   I am watching   a young couple with a small child   and a large dog   under a huge tree   in the gloaming   they become increasingly a part   of the dark   and with it   freed from form.

In 1857, he set about the many years of cut grass, carved paths, a lake designed as a choir—he ran a lot of tests and determined that music carries best over water, but this was much later, Music Island, Prospect Park, 1866.

It was a matter of addressing each sense on its own terms. He thought about the sound, of a skate across ice, of wind in a sail, of a veil in another wind, and what was thought not quite audible held scent that best composed the great range unframed, the emptied host of place opening like arms, an inner horizon, he squinted and saw, from a slight rise, the ghosts of hundreds of trees walking off in a quiet line.

Just whistle, he thought, and they'll turn around and look softly back and softly turn around again and continue on, while he painted the real ones   each with a brush   the size of a leaf the trees he planned by hand   into a trick of shadow   amid

a world that unfurled   another trick   within the sun that turned into another curve   making the fields feel larger than they really were or were ever likely to be.

Central Park: 1857-1863: 240,000 trees   millions and millions of leaves, hundreds of thousands of shades of green.

Olmsted's career in landscape architecture is usually considered to have started with Central Park, but in fact, it had its roots years earlier when, on a walking tour with friends, he'd visited Birkenhead Park in Liverpool, the first park in England built with public funds. He was struck by the fact that an entire city had seen the value, among all pastures, of the gamut of classes walking slowly with time to look only at a bird or a stream.

Olmsted's dream was, above all, to create the stage set for an egalitarian democracy, and it was largely successful. The lake turned out to be one of its most popular features. It was the element that opened Central Park on December 11, 1858, with ice-skating, which instantly became all the rage—

There, on the slipperiest of surfaces, all classes literally slid in and out of each other. Some came with their footmen; others were footmen on their day off, while others came from factory work or any number of other occupations, and it was one of the few situations at the time in which men and women could meet unchaperoned.

Two million people visited Central Park during its first year, at times up to 100,000 a day. By the 1870s, it was up to ten million a year, all of them, whether they knew it or not, struck by the fact that a park does not import into the city anything alien to it, but instead proves that open meadows, sculpted forests, expansive flowers, flowering plums, and sailboats for rent are all innate aspects of urbanity.

And encourage alterity, errancy, all the benefits of getting lost: *Such spaces will we make public and encourage the people to come here to let their minds wander.* Wander is the heart on saunter, echoing Thoreau's etymology: *saunter* as *sans terre,* as in without land to call my own, so I call it everyone's, now come home—again to amble   as a park always does, out of itself, and

must in fact, exceed its forms, its terms, its time; it's the nature of growth; landscape architecture is the only form of art that necessarily destroys itself. The exuberant grief of trees exploding so slowly in time-lapse films—Olmsted in his earliest notes: *In laying out Central Park, we determined to think of no result to be realized in less than forty years.*

If growth = overflow = what can color do to a spiral in the season, to a palace of reticence held in hushed grasses, and the tendency of his projects themselves to overflow, for instance, into city planning, such as the Riverside housing development outside of Chicago, with its 7,000 evergreens, 32,000 deciduous trees, 47,000 bushes and no streets that were not curved.

He also invented the parkway, seeing a park not only as a place to go, but also as a way of getting there. The first one was in Brooklyn, a park 260 feet wide and six miles long, from Prospect Park to Coney Island, followed by one in Buffalo, where three parks were linked by parkways, and the lots along them, sold to fund the whole thing.

Boston 1878: a series of greens with an arboretum and landscaped waterways, all linked into a system called the Emerald Necklace: the park not as an isolated instance, but as a continuum, a growing organism, a living thing sprouting extensions. In order to underscore its organic nature, he stipulated that the grass in the Franklin Park section be mowed, not by machines, but by grazing sheep.

In another section, common citizenry glided from meadow to meadow in wooden boats beneath colorful awnings, enlarging the view by sowing their attention throughout droves of roses and an activated kinetic—earlier, in Central Park, he'd taken into account the way that a body moves through the staccato of the Ramble vs the fluency of fields, more fluidly arranged according to the color of the birds they attract, the bees in aerial harbor, and the smell of just-cut grass.

In Olmsted's words: *a sense of enlarged freedom* as if freedom were a matter of the size of a vault in the sky arched by branches and paved in isinglass. One walks inside, and the self overflows, becomes an exterior thing—this is a park,

As the edges
ease in the distance, where does the tree become the breeze, the line between lake and sky compromised, quietly, and the others one passes, at times without a glance.

A park is a single organism, and everyone in it, walking through it or stopping for an hour for a picnic is one of its organs, part of its circulatory system, as well as its nerves and senses While someone standing in the window of an apartment across the street sees just one huge green being being at home.

As if art took part in leaf and took the leaf apart tree by tree. Plant the trees in strands and hold them into groves and hold the groves at glade's length and in such ways would a thousand acres pass. We walked across sunlight and then across rain, which too was blooming exactly as planned.

Christo & Jeanne-Claude
The Running Fence

"Like the tied-back curtain to a summer window" said the *Tomales Bay Times*, while the Environmental Impact Report compared it to a county fair. A flare. A flair. An unfurl. That flew.

A kite 25 miles in flight. Ignited by the sun. How did the birds respond? Especially the raptors and vultures who spend their lives riding the currents of air, showing that the atmosphere is also constructed

of hills, slopes, curves, valleys, moving not unlike the fence in its slow streak of geographic sweep, a lighthouse drawn with a long phosphorescent brush—what did it look like in the moonlight? What did it look like from the moon? And then suddenly all the animals for miles around, awake. Making a thin line drawn in lime arrive at a great wall that walled nothing in

It took four years of fighting authorities at all levels—individual, local, county, state, and federal—to get the permission. One of the recurrent complaints was extravagance—millions of dollars for a completely useless work of art that most people couldn't even bring themselves to call art. But far from being wasted, all those millions were earned by someone—engineers, manufacturers, planners, measurers, cutters, sewers, builders, drivers, monitors, photographers, and ranchers who all contributed to its creation— and a good many of them were local; it created a small economic boom in the region.

The four years of negotiation were above all about getting the agreement of the community, a community that the project built by bringing them all together around the work; in short, the community that was created by creating the art was a central element of that art; it didn't make it—it was it.

Including even the people who opposed it. If you were there at all you couldn't *not* be a part of it; you played a role in the continually unspooling theater, and in that way their work is completely realist.

The artwork: all their projects underscored the fact that art is *work*— the muscle, the logistics, the technics; it all required tremendous effort, and much of it, so physical, even dangerous. Their projects exaggerated this almost to the point of the ridiculous, reminding us that most people think of art and work as, if not diametrically opposed, at least unrelated.

Jeanne-Claude and Christo were born on the same day— June 13, 1935—she in Morocco and he in Bulgaria. They both separately said that the *Running Fence* had no beginning and no end, just two extremes—and no end either in perspectives, angles, speeds, no end to its seeing nor to its being seen. The only beginning or end it had was temporal, and that was absolute, and imbedded in its very title: *Running Fence, Sonoma and Marin Counties, California, 1972-76*—it began when they first got the idea, and it ended only once every trace of it had been removed by Oct. 31, 1976.

All of Christo and Jeanne-Claude's projects had an elaborate ephemerality at the core, endless effort spent on a glance, the eons each second takes to let this smoke go up in proof; a glimpse, one said, centers the eye's corner. I was driving by, and out of the corner of my eye, I saw flight fly.

And I, too, used to fly, said the rancher with a new-born calf in his arms, for whole split-seconds; it was the land that did it. Flight as extension, a connection that lets time touch time across time.

Flight as a muscular memory, lodged in muscles we no longer own. Or flight as a function of the eye, lifting the body beyond its possibility.

Or flight as an aberration of the eye in conjunction with an hallucination of the spine. Flight: we flew, and it was simply that; it's simply something that happens to a body in time.

And it happened again and again. "When I said that the fence flew, we flew, and so I said it again and again "

Can it be a fence if it holds nothing in? And what does it mean to run? Sheep slipping through the slits made especially for them and their freedom of movement—and their likely opinion on fences and their definitions. Not to mention the white-on-white of their wool against the cloth, a kind of Ryman in a motion of constant recomposition until it's gone. It was built to come and go—fog and mist—then lift—*voile*—veil and sail all at once until it's gone again.

How quick a streak might cause a heart—that a heart might see a quick streak take off   from it, the heart   already thought out

in light. It seems that the eye can't help but follow any bright extension   seems to leave   all boundaries in shreds.

Christo's land-into-landscape work began when he was an art student in Bulgaria—the students were sent out on the weekends to "beautify" the land through which the Orient Express passed. It was the only part of the Eastern Bloc that, at that time, the outside world could see. They were ordered to paint villages, plant flowers, pose perfect tractors attractively. *We told the peasants they should set this threshing-machine clearly silhouetted at the top of a little hill—as if on a pedestal.*

Jeanne-Claude: *I became an artist for love of Christo. If he'd been a dentist, I'd have become a dentist.*

The plans and drawings for the *Running Fence* were conceived and executed as completely separate artworks, and their sales financed the entire construction of the *Fence* itself. This was true for all of their projects; each one was funded by the sale of hundreds of plans, sketches, perspectives, and imagined depictions of the "final project." Not only did this keep them completely financially independent, but, more importantly, it confused/diffused the frame, let it overflow into a network, which is the truest form of each of their pieces: a whole, but made up of countless cells that are all wholes in themselves.

The two-dimensional works, stunning landscape sketches, are often anchored by measurements, technical notations, ordinance maps, and hand-written descriptions as aesthetically compelling as the drawings themselves. His handwriting becomes yet another ridge-line, a transcription of distance into an arboreal syntax.

And the *Fence* was, in fact, referred to by more than one commentator in terms of language. It was called a calligraphy; a hand writes, and the writing crosses, crossing evenly the line between sight and blinding—a certain second of sun—it would depend on the moment, there were moments they said, when you couldn't even look at it or you'd have a blind spot or rather a long blinding sheaf that stayed on, moving through your mind.

If we think of it as exactly that, a blind spot of interminable length a landscape of late summer   equally struck   landscape of the late suddenly thinking: Fence as frame: Walk we all in together again

walk the across—the fox   the deer   the sheep   the lost. The *Fence* holds them all, not through containment but like a magnet or mirror mirroring every angle of weather, every errant ray of cloud and all that rain that sunned inside. So many writings on the work mention rain and wind, and the shadows, cut out, sharp, of trees or cows or whatever was passing in a magic lantern, but for the facts:

165,000 yards of woven white cloth.

2,050 poles.

90 miles of steel cable.

350,000 hooks.

59 ranchers whose land the *Fence* needed to cross and who were at first so resistant.

The countless visits to all of them until one handed him a beer and invited him in. There's an art to going back again and again, to the sooner or later you'll not only agree but will become an advocate, will argue for the project in countless public meetings, with city councils, county planning commissions, and people generally difficult. And in this way, relatively conservative ranchers became outspoken advocates of avant-garde art.

In the long run, they ended up inadvertently functioning as museum guides, pointing out particularly striking perspectives, praising the aesthetics, and detailing the technical challenges that, once surmounted, made the whole thing fly. The work of art is to prove that the earth really moves, and suddenly, it's been going on for centuries   and always   a hawk

swooping exactly parallel to the undulations of the ridge, who then turned sharply down to follow the fall, was a red-tail that struck, was a feather, which might wander, or figure

the hawk gone horizontal, his wingtip of chalk tracing the waves of land, comes back in droves; they say *rolling* hills   they say *roll* and there's a long low gravel sound, calm in the face of the equally rolling sun. The *Fence* is the gesture that changes the site from land into landscape; by placing a work of art in it, it's suddenly apparent.

And you, writing out the museum label, list the materials: *light, time, and weather*, all the while thinking of the unidentifiable animal that you saw last night silhouetted against it.

Notes

Other than titles, foreign words, and self-referential words, all phrases or passages in italics are the words, either written or spoken, of the artists referenced or of someone interviewing them or writing on or to them. In a few cases, such as the titles listed in the piece on Agnes Martin and in sections of the pieces on Tacita Dean and Gustav Klimt, the artists' words have been cut up and rearranged.

Phrases in quotation marks, on the other hand, are entirely imagined and/or invented statements, even though they may seem to be attributed to the artist or another—friend, dealer, viewer, etc.

The only exception is the line "Only beauty can save the world," which is Dostoyevsky's. In "Sally Mann: Untitled Ground," in fact, she said that "she was trying to get them to give up their ghosts," rather than their graves.

Everything else in the book is by the author.

One other note related to "Sally Mann: Untitled Ground": the date of Lincoln's Emancipation Proclamation is usually given as January 1, 1863, but in fact, the preliminary version was issued on September 22, 1862.

Acknowledgements

Warm thanks to the editors of the various journals in which these pieces first appeared, at times as extracts and often in earlier versions:

Academy of American Poets: Poem-A-Day
Berkeley Poetry Review
Colorado Review
Columbia Poetry Review
The Common
Conjunctions
Denver Quarterly
Dispatches
Free Verse
Interim
Lana Turner
The Literary Imagination
Music & Literature Magazine
Ocean State Review
Pangyrus

Paperbag
Ploughshares
Poetry Daily: What Sparks a Poem/Object Lessons

"Henry Ossawa Tanner: Night Over Night" appeared in the essay collection *21 | 19: Contemporary Poets in the 19th C. Archive*, ed. Alexandra Manglis et al, Milkweed Editions, 2019.

"Willem de Kooning: Composed Windows" and "Zao Wou-ki: Enter Weather" were commissioned for the exhibition catalogue for their joint show of abstract landscapes at the Dominique Lévy Gallery in New York in the spring of 2017.

150

"Frederick Law Olmsted: The Centrality of the Park" was written as a key-note address for the Utah Symposium in Science & Literature at the University of Utah in April, 2017.

"Gustav Klimt: Seventeen Summers" was published as a chapbook by rob mclennan at above/ground press.

"Renee Gladman: Acsemic Cities" was published in a special issue of the journal *Music & Literature* dedicated to Renee Glandman's work.

Cole Swensen is the author of 17 books of poetry, most recently *On Walking On* (Nightboat, 2017), and a collection of critical essays, *Noise That Stays Noise* (2011). Her work has been awarded the Iowa Poetry Prize, the S.F. State Poetry Center Book Award, and the National Poetry Series, and has been a finalist twice for the *L.A. Times* Book Award and once for the National Book Award. A former Guggenheim Fellow, she co-edited the Norton anthology *American Hybrid* and is the founding editor of La Presse. She has translated over twenty books of French poetry, creative non-fiction, and art criticism, including Jean Frémon's *Island of the Dead*, which won the PEN USA Award in Translation. She divides her time between Paris and Providence R.I., where she teaches at Brown University.

NIGHTBOAT BOOKS

Nightboat Books, a nonprofit organization, seeks to develop audiences for writers whose work resists convention and transcends boundaries. We publish books rich with poignancy, intelligence, and risk. Please visit nightboat.org to learn about our titles and how you can support our future publications.

The following individuals have supported the publication of this book. We thank them for their generosity and commitment to the mission of Nightboat Books:

Kazim Ali
Anonymous
Jean C. Ballantyne
Photios Giovanis
Amanda Greenberger
Elizabeth Motika
Benjamin Taylor
Peter Waldor
Jerrie Whitfield & Richard Motika

In addition, this book has been made possible, in part, by grants from National Endowment for the Arts, the New York City Department of Cultural Affairs in partnership with the City Council, and the New York State Council on the Arts Literature Program.